A DIFFERENT
KIND OF
LOVE STORY

A DIFFERENT KIND OF LOVE STORY

HOW GOD'S LOVE FOR YOU HELPS YOU LOVE YOURSELF

LANDRA YOUNG HUGHES
with HOLLY CRAWSHAW

BakerBooks
a division of Baker Publishing Group
Grand Rapids, Michigan

© 2020 by Landra Young Hughes

Published by Baker Books
a division of Baker Publishing Group
PO Box 6287, Grand Rapids, MI 49516-6287
www.bakerbooks.com

Printed in the United States of America

Library of Congress Cataloging-in-Publication Data
Library of Congress Cataloging-in-Publication Data
Names: Hughes, Landra Young, 1994– author. | Crawshaw, Holly, other.
Title: A different kind of love story : how God's love for you helps you love yourself /
    Landra Young Hughes with Holly Crawshaw.
Description: Grand Rapids, Michigan : Baker Books, a division of Baker Publishing
    Group, 2020. | Includes bibliographical references.
Identifiers: LCCN 2019039592 | ISBN 9780801094835 (paperback)
Subjects: LCSH: God (Christianity)—Love. | Self-acceptance—Religious Aspects—
    Christianity. | Self-esteem—Religious aspects—Christianity.
Classification: LCC BT140 .H84 2020 | DDC 231/.6—dc23
LC record available at https://lccn.loc.gov/2019039592

Unless otherwise indicated, Scripture quotations are from the Holy Bible, New In-ternational Reader's Version®. NIrV®. Copyright © 1995, 1996, 1998, 2014 by Biblica, Inc.™ Used by permission of Zondervan. www.zondervan.com. The "NIrV" and "New International Reader's Version" are trademarks registered in the United States Patent and Trademark Office by Biblica, Inc.™

Scripture quotations labeled NIV are from the Holy Bible, New International Ver-sion®. NIV®. Copyright © 1973, 1978, 1984, 2011 by Biblica, Inc.™ Used by permission of Zondervan. All rights reserved worldwide. www.zondervan.com. The "NIV" and "New International Version" are trademarks registered in the United States Patent and Trademark Office by Biblica, Inc.™

Scripture quotations labeled KJV are from the King James Version of the Bible.

The Author is represented by The FEDD Agency, Inc.

20 21 22 23 24 25 26   7 6 5 4 3 2 1

I dedicate this book to my precious daughter, Sterling.

May you always see and love yourself as God sees and loves you.

I will always love you with all my heart.

To : ME

CONTENTS

PREFACE

I have a confession to make.

I love *The Bachelor*.

Not, like, the literal current contestant, but the show itself. And while we're kicking things off here with brutal honesty, you should know that I also love *The Bachelorette* and even *Bachelor in Paradise*.

I can practically feel your judgment now and I probably deserve it.

But I love watching people chase love. Is there a more relatable concept? Not that we're all crossing our fingers to get an invite to a group date, but it's in our wiring to want and need human connection. And that may look different from one person to the next, but ultimately, we all want to be loved.

I left something out of my confession. I am one of those people who seriously cannot wait until the end of a series to find out who gets the final rose. That's right, guys. I READ THE SPOILERS.

I'm not sure what that says about my character, but I'm not going to stop doing it. In fact, I am going to give you a spoiler right now.

In this book, you're going to read about a different kind of love story. It's a love story each and every one of us is currently playing a role in—whether we're aware of it or not. And truth be told, it's scary critical that we stay tuned-in to this love story. Because outside of a growing relationship with God, no other love (or lack of love) has the potential to improve or implode your life like the love that you have for *you*.

That's right. This book is about learning to love yourself. And I don't mean like, go have a pedicure and a solo Target run. Those things are amazing, but they're on the surface of what it means to genuinely know, accept, and love you.

Inside these pages, you'll read about things I've done and choices I've made that I *never* thought I would share with anyone in a million years—especially the general public. I am going to reveal secrets I buried for years and years that make my *Bachelor* confession look like story time at the local library.

And while there aren't any roses in my story, there are definitely a few thorns. Throw in some media-induced drama, my personal control issues, and my entire family being deceived, and the stage is set for some quality entertainment.

So even if you don't yet see the point in reading a book on loving yourself, you should at least turn the page to see who gets the final rose.

ONE

Plot Twist

Jesus replied, "Friend, do what you came to do."

Matthew 26:50

I was sitting on a bus on the way to basketball camp, surrounded by my friends and teammates, when I got the phone call that would change everything. It was my mom.

"Whatever you do," she said, "don't watch TV. Turn off your cell phone, and don't listen to anyone who tries to talk to you about your dad."

Like a scene from *Gossip Girl*, my teammates' phones vibrated with a chorus of texts. And, yup. Their whispers and sideways glances told me what I already knew: those messages were about my dad.

I was barely fifteen years old. A freshman at a new school on the way to basketball camp. Not a care in the world beyond whether or not I would get to dress out for varsity come fall. But then, in that one single moment, everything changed.

You know what we call this in #BachelorNation? We call this a *plot twist.*

Have you ever gotten into a TV or book series, only to be blindsided by a plot twist? Things are going totally fine until the main character gets into an awful accident, becomes friends with the villain, or is killed off (I'm looking at you, *Grey's Anatomy*). When that happens, you have to wonder . . .

Is this the end of the series?

Did they just ruin the whole thing?

Whose dumb idea was this anyway?

As fun as those moments are to watch on TV, it's just different when you experience a plot twist in real life, isn't it?

Now my parents aren't, like, Jay-Z and Beyoncé–level famous, but in the church world, they're well-known as the founding pastors of Fellowship Church, a nondenominational congregation with multiple campuses across the country. My dad, Ed Young, is a communicator and leader in the church space. He's also a *New York Times* and Amazon bestselling author (no pressure, Landra) with a handful of spots on broadcast TV.

I had no clue that in my absence our privacy had been completely violated. Journalists had been secretly interviewing staff members at our church. Helicopters had circled our home taking photos. News reporters had even dug through our trash in an attempt to question my dad's integrity as the pastor of a church. Essentially, their angle was that my dad's financial success meant he was a thief. (He's not. My dad's character and work ethic are unmatched.)

My teenage mind reeled with the shocking loss of privacy and the sudden realization that my life and my family's life were being scrutinized. I mean, they took pictures of my sisters and me as if that proved something about my dad's character. They even stole flight records from the airport to see where he was flying and snuck photos of my parents' place in Miami (where the church has a campus, by the way).

Like I said, I was in ninth grade at a new school when this all went down, and to say it was a challenging time would be the understatement of the millennium. Finding out that your life is under the microscope of the mainstream media can certainly make a teenager feel overly self-conscious. In other words, it about drove me nuts.

Let's start with the betrayal. Have you ever had a friend straight up hurt you? Like, turn their back on you or reject you? (I really want to make a *Bachelor*-betrayal joke here, but I'll refrain since this part of my book should probably be treated with some seriousness and not be compared to a Molly-Jason-Melissa scenario.)

In all seriousness, it felt like those staff members who gave interviews against my dad's reputation personally shoved a knife between my shoulder blades.

And even more brutal was the backlash.

As our once-faithful church family and close friends chose to believe untrue accusations and even help spread the false rumors, the hurt continued to deepen. How could lifelong friends whom we had fought in the trenches with suddenly leave our side when we needed them most? We had visited them in the hospital, taken them meals when they were hurting, and held their hands when beloved family members passed away. But when we hoped they would stand by us, they chose to believe the lies and perpetuate the cycle of pain. The betrayal cut into my heart, and my faith in the power of friendship to help and heal took a severe blow.

Want to know who else knows something about betrayal? (Besides reality TV personalities, of course.)

You guessed it. At least, maybe you guessed it. It's Jesus.

When I think or talk about Jesus, sometimes it's hard for me to imagine him being like me. Like a human. Who, like, had bad breath and enjoyed the odd afternoon nap. But Jesus *was* like me—like us. I wrestle with his humanity more than I wrestle with his God-ness, which logically speaking doesn't make a ton of sense. There are historical records of Jesus living and walking this planet, but somehow it's more difficult for me to believe that Jesus was ticklish than it is for me to believe that Jesus beat hell, death, and the grave to rise from the dead.

The New Testament makes it clear that Jesus had a human body: "The Word became a human being" (John 1:14). Can't really argue with that, can we? We also read that Jesus was born (Luke 2:7), that he grew (Luke 2:40), and that he dealt with conditions like tiredness (John 4:6), thirst (John 19:28), and hunger (Matt. 4:2). Jesus had needs—vulnerabilities.

And if you think about it, it's Jesus's vulnerabilities that make him the *most* like us. But that's the same for all people, right? We relate best to each other when we realize we share a common experience—struggles, challenges, and setbacks.

But Jesus's vulnerabilities weren't limited to physical issues. He was emotionally vulnerable too. He was impressionable (Matt. 8:10), sorrowful (Matt. 26:38), movable (John 11:33–35), and troubled (John 13:21).

One of Jesus's most glaring vulnerabilities was a result of his very nature. Jesus was *relational*. When he came to earth, he could have chosen a number of ways to influence people. He was the Son of God—he had the ability to speak a word and command the knee of any man or woman he wanted. But that's positional influence—the influence you have over people who have less power than you. It's easy to exert positional (vertical) influence. We do this as parents every time we tell our kids, "Do it because I said so." In other words, "I am the boss, so do as I say."

No, Jesus chose the *other* type of influence—relational influence. The kind of influence that requires time, effort, and work. Jesus's influence with his disciples had everything to do with the relationship that he shared with them. They were his friends. His "ride or dies." They shared their lives together, and like with all close relationships, Jesus opened himself up to the potential for great hurt.

Enter Judas. Judas Iscariot was one of the twelve disciples Jesus chose to do life with.

You've heard this story before. But let's dig into the account together because I think there's something incredible we can learn about the character of Jesus here. You may have read that Judas disclosed Jesus's identity to the chief priests and elders for thirty pieces of silver, playing a crucial role in Jesus's apprehension and subsequent crucifixion. Here's the exact telling:

> While Jesus was still speaking, Judas arrived. He was one of the 12 disciples. A large crowd was with him. They were carrying swords and clubs. The chief priests and the elders of the people had sent them. Judas, who was going to hand Jesus over, had arranged a signal with them. "The one I kiss is the man," he said. "Arrest him." So Judas went to Jesus at once. He said, "Greetings, Rabbi!" And he kissed him. (Matt. 26:47–49)

I mean, I can think of a thousand less intimate ways that Judas could have let the crowd know who Jesus was. But Judas betrayed Jesus with *a kiss on his cheek.*

Have you ever felt that cold whisper of betrayal against your skin? Can you imagine how Jesus must have felt as Judas walked toward him, knowing full well what his friend and follower was up to?

Surely Jesus watched each of Judas's steps in torment. *Turn around, Judas. You don't have to do this, friend. Please.*

But Judas traded his friend for a fistful of coins. And Jesus knew it was coming. "Jesus replied, 'Friend, do what you came to do'" (Matt. 26:50).

FRIEND? Jesus, come on. I can think of a few words I'd use for Judas in that moment, but none of them would have been *friend.*

Maybe Jesus put a little sarcastic emphasis on the word to remind Judas *just* whose death warrant he'd signed. Chances are, he didn't. Because if you've ever had the breath knocked out of you by someone you love hurting you, you know those initial moments of shock can be a slow ache. An ache of disbelief. An ache of sorrow. Of loss.

It's the same ache I felt in the backlash of my family being betrayed.

Friend, do what you came to do.

Jesus looked in the cold face of deception, the face of a man he loved—a man whom he'd done *life* with—and had a choice as to how he was going to react. He chose compassion.

Here's a freebie: when we have a choice between compassion and anything else, Jesus wants us to choose compassion.

In the following weeks, I would like to say I chose compassion. But I didn't. My problem on that bus in ninth grade was less about my lack of compassion toward others and more about my lack of compassion toward myself. I withdrew. I shut down.

And it was during this season of emotional pandemonium that I first developed the symptoms of a disease that would nearly destroy my body and my life.

You see, I am currently in recovery for a severe eating disorder that includes behaviors associated with anorexia, bulimia, and bingeing and purging. An eating disorder whose roots sprang to life when the news stories about my dad broke. At that point, I officially lost *control*. I didn't have control over who took my photo. I didn't have control over what my friends said about me when I wasn't in the room. It felt like I didn't have control over *anything*.

Except what I ate. I controlled precious little—but I did control that.

Because when you're a teenager, there's no one making airplane noises with a bright red spoon, forcing you to take bites of food. And if there is someone watching you eat, you can always get rid of it (purge) later.

In the wake of what felt like universal rejection, a deep cavern had been carved into my newly wounded heart. A place I knew logically Jesus *wanted* to fill. Because he loves me no matter what, right? That's what I had been told my whole life.

The problem was, I felt ashamed. I felt angry. I felt alone and unlovable.

My eating disorder became my comfort. My safe place. My friend. And in a twisted sense, it became my way of feeling loved.

Can anyone else relate to that? To turning to sources you know will hurt you as a way of making yourself feel better?

Maybe for you it's alcohol, or overeating, or overspending, or even overthinking. We use these things like pacifiers when we feel out of control, disappointed, rejected, or hurt.

And that's because we're all looking for the same thing—*to be loved*. To be loved with a different kind of love than the imperfect variety that we experience in our earthly relationships.

One of my favorite movies is James Cameron's *Avatar*. If you've never seen it, it's about the alien world of Pandora and its inhabitants, the Na'Vi beings. If you have seen it, how are the blue Na'Vi people still so gorgeous? I don't know how the filmmakers did it—but the graphics are breathtaking.

Back to the point.

One of the Na'Vi greetings is *Oel ngati kameie*, or *I see you*.[1]

I see you.

I comprehend you.

I understand you.

I see you—not just on the outside but on the inside too.

I think it's one of the most beautiful expressions I've ever heard. *That's* what we long for—to be *seen* by someone. To be seen and known but still be fully accepted.

That's the different kind of love our Creator made us to crave.

So let me pose this question: Why would God design us to want something that we can't find on this side of heaven?

Did he want to set us up for disappointment?

Did he want to test our ability to withstand hurt?

Did he want us all to get repeated concussions from banging our heads against walls out of frustration and despair?

Here's what *I* believe God was thinking when he wired us with the desire to be loved unconditionally: God created us to want to be loved in a way only he can love because he's jealous for our hearts.

That may sound "churchy." Or maybe it just sounds straight up weird. But it's true—God wants to be the only one who is able to meet that innate need because he wants to hold a piece of our hearts that no one else can touch.

And when we try to fit other things inside that God-shaped hole?

In my case, it spelled complete and utter disaster.

TWO

Jesus Take the Wheel

In their hearts human beings plan their lives. But the LORD decides where their steps will take them.

Proverbs 16:9

You know what really burns my metaphorical biscuits?

Movies that end in a huge, shocking reveal that changes the entire context of everything that's come before the revelation.

For example, I remember watching *The Sixth Sense* with Bruce Willis for the first time. In the movie, a young Haley Joel Osment begins working with a therapist (Bruce Willis) after having some unsettling experiences with ghosts he's been seeing. Then, in the last few minutes of the film, it's revealed that Bruce Willis was *ACTUALLY* DEAD THE ENTIRE TIME. HE WAS JUST ANOTHER GHOST HALEY JOEL OSMENT HAD BEEN SEEING.

Talk about a plot twist!

When the movie ended, I immediately wanted to go back and watch it all over again to look for clues that Bruce wasn't the living, breathing counselor I fully believed he was 129 of the 130 minutes of the movie.

I literally sat on my parents' sofa with my mouth hanging open, staring at the blank TV like someone had just pulled a huge prank on me.

The truth is, there have been many moments where I've felt the same way about my own life. Like a twist in the plot just ruined the whole story. Like nothing will ever be okay again. That's definitely how I felt after the news outlets released the story about my family.

Not to be a Debbie Downer over here, but if you haven't had that experience yet, it's coming. It's a part of life. There's going to be a time, there's been a time in the past, or you're in a time right now where it feels like God has written one huge plot twist into the script of your life.

Things are going great until something happens that completely stops you in your tracks.

Maybe for you it was when . . .

- you were dumped
- you lost your job
- you lost the baby unexpectedly
- someone close to you died
- your child made a decision that broke your heart

Or maybe it wasn't just *one* moment or thing that happened. Instead, it's an ongoing set of disappointing circumstances—things that you didn't sign up for that seem to have no end in sight. Things like:

- chronic infertility
- an anxiety or depression diagnosis
- mounting debt
- a sickness that won't go away

Or maybe it's something completely different. It doesn't have to be dramatic or motion-picture worthy, but nearly all of us experience something that is disappointing, painful, or just a huge letdown.

Sometimes we know what we could do to make the situation better. But more often, we don't know where to start. We feel powerless to do anything at all. Or we cope by doing something unhealthy that eventually leads to even more problems. For me, it was an eating disorder. Maybe you've chosen your own bad habit.

It's a miserable place to be, but what other choice do we have? When we can't fix the situation, and we don't want to fake being happy about it, is being miserable really our only option?

Before we unpack all this, I want you to know that if you've ever felt a bit helpless or hopeless, or you're feeling that way now, it's okay. When bad things happen, it's okay to feel bad about them. It'd be weird if you didn't. You're not the only person to feel that way, and you're certainly not the first. You're normal. (Sometimes I need to hear that reminder. We. Are. Normal.)

Since the very beginning of time, people have experienced disappointments and struggled to figure out what to do with them. Even after Jesus came, that was true. And for one of his followers, Paul, it was especially true.

Paul was no stranger to the feeling of loss or disappointment. If you're not familiar with his story, let me catch you up for a second.

Paul experienced a huge plot twist—a good one, though it was earth-shattering for him at the time—when he met Jesus. Maybe I should mention that, at that point, Jesus had already died and had risen from the dead. Like I said, *plot twist*. That encounter changed Paul's life so much that he went from plotting to murder Jesus's followers to becoming one of them. His life did a 180.

In fact, not only was Paul a follower but he also became a missionary and a leader who wrote letters to other groups of Jesus followers, instructing them and encouraging them. Those letters make up a large part of what we call the New Testament.

But becoming a Jesus follower didn't exactly make Paul popular with everyone. In one of his letters to a group of friends in Corinth, he wrote, "Three times I was beaten with rods, once I was pelted with stones, three times I was shipwrecked, I spent a night and a day in the open sea" (2 Cor. 11:25 NIV).

Beaten and shipwrecked, Paul found himself in all sorts of disappointing positions. So when he wrote to his friends in the church at Corinth about how to handle tough circumstances, he wasn't speaking as an outsider or someone with an easy life. He was speaking as an expert. And the advice he gave can help you and me as we figure out what to do with some of life's toughest circumstances.

> We are pushed hard from all sides. But we are not beaten down. We are bewildered. But that doesn't make us lose hope. Others

make us suffer. But God does not desert us. We are knocked down. But we are not knocked out. (2 Cor. 4:8–9)

Notice what Paul *didn't* say. He didn't say, "Everything is fine." He didn't pretend that life for Jesus followers is awesome and fun and easy all the time. No, Paul came right out of the gate describing just how bad things really were for them. And maybe the way he described it sounds familiar to you. Maybe you know what it feels like when trouble comes from "all sides," or you feel perplexed and confused, bullied or knocked down in life. Paul made an interesting point here. He said, "We are pushed hard from all sides. But we are not beaten down" (v. 8).

Sometimes when we experience tough times or letdowns in our lives, we feel like they'll be the *end* of us. In the wake of the news story, I would find myself making extreme statements like:

My life is over.

It'll never get better.

Now I'll never be able to . . .

But Paul is saying that just because a situation stinks—and things *definitely* stink—doesn't mean it's the end of the story. We're pushed hard on all sides . . . but not beaten down. Perplexed (or confused) . . . but not in despair. Knocked down . . . but not destroyed.

In other words, there may have been a plot twist, but we don't know the end of the story. Just because something is bad doesn't mean life is bad. And it doesn't mean things can't get better.

In such a rough time in life, how could Paul say something like that? Why did he seem so sure, so hopeful that, while the situation was bad, it wasn't the end? There's a clue in something Paul said only a few verses later.

> So we don't spend all our time looking at what we can see. Instead, we look at what we can't see. That's because what can be seen lasts only a short time. But what can't be seen will last forever. (2 Cor. 4:18)

Paul understood that there was always more to the situation than what he could see. And he chose to fix his eyes—and focus his mind—on the fact that God was at work, even when it didn't feel like it. And that's true for your situation too. Even when there's trouble, you can trust him.

You can choose to fix your mind on the trouble in front of you. You can convince yourself that your life is over. Or you can fix your mind on the fact that there's a God who loves you, who is all-powerful, and who is up to something that you might not be able to see *just yet*.

When you fix your mind on what is unseen, you can begin to experience the same thing that led Paul to write this letter—hope. And not just hope that things will get better but hope that even if things don't ever go the way you want them to, you'll be okay. Your story isn't over and you can have hope that even when there's trouble, God can be trusted to get you through it to what comes next.

When you experience tough times, it can be easy to convince yourself that you'll never get over it or you'll never be okay again. And while it's normal to feel that way for a while, you have to avoid getting stuck there. Like Paul, you can choose where to focus your attention. You can fix your mind on the trouble in front of you or you can focus on . . .

What you know to be true about God. What have you learned about God from the Bible, from your small group, or from your own personal experience with him? Have you learned that he is loving? That he is powerful? That he is kind toward you? Focus on those things. For example, search for verses that talk about his character and his love for you, and make those the lock screen on your phone. Plug them in as reminders in your calendar. Or find other creative ways to remind yourself that even when there's trouble, God can be trusted.

Where you've seen him at work before. Have you already seen ways that God has taken care of you? Ways that he has been trustworthy in your life? Maybe it's in your personal life or maybe it's in the life of someone you know. Maybe it's in a story you heard. God is always up to something. Pay attention to the areas where he is working, and focus your mind on those. That'll make it easier to trust him in the areas where his plan isn't so obvious.

Where he could use this pain in your life or in the world around you. Is there a way that God could use your pain and tough circumstances to grow you? Or is there a way that you can imagine God using your circumstance to help someone else in the future? If so, focus on that. It won't make your situation easy, and it won't make it go away. But when you know that what you're experiencing right now, as hard as it is, could benefit someone else in a similar situation later, it may give you the strength you need to get through it. Even when it's painful, God can use the most awful situations in your life to help you or help others.

Listen, I know this is easier said than done—and I also know that some of you aren't sure whether you believe in God or the Bible—but I want you to know that no matter what you believe about him, God is still there for you. He loves you and can be trusted to get you through all of life's hardest circumstances. It's because of him that you can be: pressed . . . but not crushed; perplexed . . . but not in despair; and knocked down . . . but not destroyed.

Sometimes things happen that throw you for a loop. But no situation, loss, or difficult circumstance has the final say in your life. Like Paul, you can go through hard times without letting them get the best of you as you keep your eyes on your heavenly Father who loves you. Even when there's trouble, you can trust him.

As you head out today, I want you to think of one situation in your life that has the tendency to get you down. What would it look like for you to choose to trust God in that area? I know this book would be more salacious (I really wanted to say "juicy" but that's just kind of a weird word, right? Thesaurus .com FTW!) if I told you that my parents reacted dramatically to the media explosion.

Mom put on her finest silk robe and locked herself in the bathroom while Dad wiped his tears with hundred dollar bills.

Nope. My parents took the indictment of their character on the chin. They displayed the same grace and integrity that I had witnessed my entire life.

My dad chose to stand strong, believing God's truth that he would see us through this trial. In the same way, my mom carried on with her beautiful balance of rock-solid stability and the sensitivity to reach out to others and help them. She firmly trusted God and encouraged my sisters, brother, and me to do the same.

Their mission became helping us find joy and ways to laugh no matter how difficult the circumstances became.

Now my parents aren't robots. I am sure they were hurt and angry in ways they never expressed to my siblings and me. But how they felt on the inside is not how they reacted on the outside. While their insides were probably screaming, *Why, God, why?*, their words and actions said *peace*.

Are you a heart-on-your-sleeve kind of person? I am. I sing this song to my almost-two-year-old daughter, Sterling, all the time: "If you're happy and you know it, clap your hands! If you're happy and you know it, then your face will surely show it."

Yeah. That's me. If I am happy, mad, sad, angry, or confused—my face will surely show it. But my parents? See, they had been *practicing* the discipline of not allowing their emotions to dictate their behavior.

My parents spent years studying and embracing God's peace until it was just part of their DNA. They experienced countless hardships but God carried them through time after time. They use these stories as evidence of God's goodness when they encounter what we might view as chaos.

A perfect example of this is when my dad was teaching pastor in his father's successful church, but God called him to leave his dream job behind for a different plan. Not even thirty years old, he had everything he could want—working for his dad in a stable work environment with close friends and solid mentors—yet when God told him to move to Grapevine, Texas, to start a church, my dad trusted the plan. He gave up preaching in a beautiful church to minister out of a rented office complex with a small congregation. The move didn't seem to make sense, but within a few years, the church grew to over five thousand members. In less than a decade, the church moved from the office to a school auditorium and then to a property of over a hundred and forty acres. As I write this today, the church ministers to over twenty thousand congregants across nine campuses. But what's more important are the countless lives that have been changed in immeasurable ways because my parents chose the chaos of the unknown over the comfort of the known.

My parents had no clue where God was leading them when they first moved, but they gave him complete control and watched as his plans exceeded their expectations.

See, there's a difference between feeling something and letting that something control your life.

Think of it this way.

View your life as a car with multiple passengers. Fear's there. Anxiety. Shame. Self-loathing. Your past. Anger, hurt, regret. But there's also *God's truth*. When it's time to get in that car and go, you have a choice about who is driving. You can always let your emotions take the wheel. (And I'll be honest, sometimes I do.) But they might lead you down a dead-end street in the middle of nowhere and you'll have to circle right back to where you started from.

But anytime I let God's truth about me and who he says I am drive my words, thoughts, and actions, the road is always easier. It's not without its potholes, detours, or traffic jams, but I get where I need to go.

Here's what the Bible says on the matter: "In their hearts human beings plan their lives. But the LORD decides where their steps will take them" (Prov. 16:9).

The thing is, God is going to chase us down. We can try to plan our lives and let our emotions control us, but we can't outrace God.

I know what you're thinking. (Or singing.)

Jesus take the wheeeeeeeeeeel!

But, really, letting Jesus take the wheel will protect us from future hurt and regret. During the aftermath of THE story, my parents put their emotions in the back seat and just let God drive. When it surfaced on the nightly news, I wish I could say I chose to relax and embrace the idea that "God's got this." But I didn't. Rather than give God control, I decided to focus on the few things I could control: I could strictly manage exactly what I ate and how much I ate. And I became very good at it.

I have always had an athletic build—perfect for when I was competing for a spot on the varsity basketball team as a freshman in high school, but not perfect when I tried on clothes and wanted to look like the slimmer girls I saw at school and on social media. There had always been a whisper in my head saying, *If you were thinner, you would be more attractive. If you were more attractive, more people would like you. If more people liked you, you would be happier.*

Isn't the enemy shrewd in his lies? Say what you want about the devil, but he is a smart adversary. He never takes us down an illogical path. In our minds, his deception makes perfect sense. He starts with a thought that leads to another thought that leads to another thought . . . and on the surface it all sounds so *true*. So *obvious*.

And I believed every word of his lies.

At the heart of my eating disorder was control. It was my way of coping with the stress of the news story and the betrayal of friends. Controlling what I ate felt like security. I could even manipulate the truth and hold the key to my secret.

"Oh, no thanks. I am not hungry. I just had a big lunch at my parents' house."

Except that I hadn't.

"Wow, I am super full. I just had the best cheesecake at the restaurant. I can't believe I ate two whole slices."

Except that wasn't true either.

I was endlessly pushing food around my plate and claiming I was taking it all home to eat later as leftovers.

Of course the compliments on my appearance didn't hurt. While insecurity and hurt fueled my addiction to starving, the immediate gratification I received from others continued to feed it too.

"You look great, Landra! Have you lost weight?"

"What workouts are you doing? Share your secret!"

Want to know how bad it got? At a certain point, I was only eating four saltine crackers and seven raspberries a day. I currently feed my toddler more than that at any given snack time.

The problem with instant gratification is that it is *so* instantly gratifying. In the moment, it feels so good. The control and affirmation I experienced during my eating disorder were emotional Band-Aids to a gaping wound that really needed surgery.

Maybe you've done that before—you've done what you could to cope in the short term to avoid the potential of hurting in the long term. Maybe your Band-Aid was a rebound relationship. A shopping habit. An extra glass (or four) of wine. Helicopter parenting. Spending too much time at work.

Have you ever tried to walk on a sprained ankle before it healed? Needed stitches but didn't get them? Went to the gym too soon after an illness? When we don't allow our bodies the time they need to recover, it can often exacerbate our symptoms or end up making us feel worse.

In their hearts human beings plan their lives.

We try to plan our lives. We set expectations. We get our hopes up. And when we feel rejected or disappointed, we spiral. Because we don't plan for *those* things.

But the LORD decides where their steps will take them.

We can let anything—hurt, fear, our own will—drive our lives, but ultimately, God decides where we're going. He's not surprised by our choices or by the choices of those around us. Even when they don't make sense to us, God sees the turns ahead.

So when we settle for instant gratification and Band-Aid reactions, God whispers to us, *I want to take you somewhere different. It's a little farther down the road, but it's worth the drive.*

God wants to take us somewhere we can be fully healed and well to live out his perfect plan for our lives.

In hindsight, that makes a lot of sense. Back when I started controlling my eating habits so severely, I knew I was only hurting myself more. But once I started down the slippery slope of secret sin, it felt like I couldn't stop.

THREE

Secrets Don't Make Friends

Don't you know that your bodies are temples of the Holy Spirit?
The Spirit is in you, and you have received the Spirit from God.
You do not belong to yourselves. Christ has paid the price for
you. So use your bodies in a way that honors God.

1 Corinthians 6:19–20

I remember the first time I felt skinny. Like *really* skinny. I was a
teenager, about seventeen, and I had just had my wisdom teeth
removed. My cheeks were so swollen that I looked like a chipmunk that had tried to swallow another chipmunk, but I woke
up one morning and noticed something else about my body had
changed. My sweatpants were loose, fitting me more like they
would fit my sister. (We are twins, but she is naturally thinner.)

This moment is etched in my mind as the catalyst for what
would follow.

I checked myself out in the mirror.

I was thinner.

Because of my dental work, I hadn't been able to eat much at all. And what I had eaten was liquid and minimal.

I don't know if I decided that very second to keep up the new-found eating patterns, but that's exactly what I did. I restricted myself to very little food—the more liquids, the better and the less I ate, the better. And I was right—I continued to lose weight.

It didn't seem like a big deal at the time. But what sin starts off as a huge problem?

Is having an eating disorder a sin?

Yeah, I wasn't going to drop that bomb at the end of the last chapter and just leave you hanging with it. My answer to that question is complicated. I can only speak for myself, but here's how I view it.

Anything that makes you lie to people who love you, encourages you to hurt yourself and endanger your health, or steals your joy and controls your life probably (most definitely) falls into the category of sin.

The Bible really doesn't leave any question:

> Don't you know that your bodies are temples of the Holy Spirit? The Spirit is in you, and you have received the Spirit from God. You do not belong to yourselves. Christ has paid the price for you. So use your bodies in a way that honors God. (1 Cor. 6:19–20)

Anytime we abuse our bodies (as we often do in the name of busyness, vanity, or depression), we are defying the Word of God. Our bodies do not belong to us. They were purchased, bought for an extremely high price—the life of Jesus.

Do you own anything of great value? A house? A car? A family heirloom? An expensive piece of jewelry? A phone or tablet? A scrapbook of your child's first year?

Chances are, you take care of the things you value. Maybe you keep them in a safe. Or a protective case. You may handle them with the utmost care and would never *ever* consider tossing them in the trash can or leaving them out in the rain. They matter too much to you.

But when it comes to how we treat ourselves—internally and externally—it's a different story.

Why is that? Because nothing we own on this earth came at a higher price than our own lives.

I wish I had grasped this truth earlier. I wish I hadn't let my eating disorder rob me of years' worth of joy, trust, and connection. But it did.

I restricted my eating even further. At one point, I was eating just a few nuts throughout the day to keep myself alive.

That's when the bingeing started. At first, it was involuntary.

I would go on a trip with my family and tell myself I could eat like a "regular person" for one day of that trip. It was a treat to myself, and it threw my family off their suspicions that I was as sick as I was.

The only problem with that plan was that I was literally *starving*. And once I started eating, I couldn't stop. I would wake up in the middle of the night and my body would be super angry at me. I would throw up everything in my stomach until there was literally nothing left.

But then I got an idea. What if I ate *on purpose* on the days I couldn't stand the hunger any longer and made myself throw up *on purpose* to get rid of it once my appetite was satiated?

That's how the cycle of bingeing and purging started.

Days of starvation. A binge day. Throw up. Then more days of starvation to punish myself for indulging.

It wasn't long into my illness that the compliments turned to true concern.

"Are you *still* losing weight?"

"That dress looks huge on you."

"Are you getting enough to eat?"

Then my mom forced me to go to my pediatrician. I'll never forget the look on her face when she assessed me, asking me what felt like a hundred questions—none of which I answered with complete honesty.

She studied me briefly.

"You have an eating disorder, Landra," she said. "A severe one." She stared at me for a few tense moments. Then she said, "You may die from this."

I wish her warning had been enough to make me stop. But my addiction had become the only thing I felt connected to. The only way I felt security. I knew in my brain that God was screaming at me, begging for me to bring my hurt and pain to him for true healing. But I didn't listen.

It's ironic how you develop a secret like an addiction because you feel so alone. Because it only serves to isolate you further, exacerbating all the symptoms you're trying to escape.

Let's talk about secrets for a minute. Now, I am not talking about *surprises*. I love surprises like cupcakes, parties, flowers, jewelry, guest appearances on the Women Tell All episode.

But secrets are not surprises. Secrets are the things we actively try to hide to protect ourselves or someone else. Now I believe that everybody has at least one secret. The tricky thing about secrets is that they always start off fun.

"Texting him is harmless. It's not going to go anywhere."

"I'll stop for one drink before I go home. I deserve it."

"Hiding receipts isn't a big deal. Everybody does it."

Think about your favorite restaurant at night. The dim lighting glimmers from the ceiling. Gorgeous, plush booths with slick leather chairs. The tables sparkle. The music is perfect. The atmosphere is absolutely mesmerizing.

But if you were to go to that restaurant before it opens at eight, you'd be shocked.

The lights are turned all the way up. The music is turned all the way down.

A thin film of grease covers everything.

The carpet looks threadbare and stained.

The décor is dated and the framed art is speckled with a mystery sauce.

Rush-hour traffic blares in the background.

It looks completely different.

That's how secrets work. When a secret is a secret—when it's in the dark—it's mysterious. It's alluring. It's fun.

But when a secret is brought into the light, you can see it for what it really is.

A mirage.

An illusion.

The worst kind of trick.

I mean, we don't really enjoy it when people we love keep secrets from us, right? (Remember, a *surprise* is different from a *secret*.) We don't even enjoy it when people we *don't* love keep secrets from us.

Think about it. When's the last time a headline read "Politician's Secret Exposed and No One Cares" or "Affair Revealed and No One Got Hurt"? How about "Man Has Secret Baby with Mistress and Wife Shrugs Her Shoulders"?

Secrets *hurt*. They hurt us and they hurt those around us.

The thing is, when the secrets are *our* secrets, it doesn't always *feel* like they're hurting anyone. Maybe we're aware that the things we harbor are potentially harmful to ourselves, but we will also use any excuse possible to justify our hidden actions.

"Well, the marriage was dead anyway."

"They're so rich, they'll never miss the money."

"Who cares how much I drink?"

"This isn't a big deal."

"It's my body. My life. I should be able to do what I want."

"If I can make this go away without anyone finding out, no one will get hurt."

Or the lie I told myself about my secret: *I am only hurting myself. So it doesn't matter what anyone else thinks.*

Here's the thing. Secrets make us sick. Secrets draw us out of the light and into the dark.

My husband, Brad, and I recently moved to Oklahoma. A few weeks ago, our power went out in the middle of dinner. Has that ever happened to you? To make matters worse, it was dark outside. I couldn't see anything, and I didn't have my phone close by to use as a flashlight. (I am so bad about having my phone on me. I may be known as the World's Worst Texter Backer.) So Brad and I were feeling around in our new house, trying to find a candle, a lighter, a flashlight—anything to bring some light into the room. Of course Sterling thought it was all hilarious, but I was starting to panic.

So I grabbed Sterling (who literally could not have cared less that the lights were off—homegirl was still shoveling food in her mouth as I lifted her from the high chair) and tried to picture the last place I saw any source of light. As I rounded the corner from the kitchen into the den, I took what I judged to be a totally safe step.

Only it was not a safe step.

Would you believe that the coffee table shifted on its own and slammed itself into my shin? No? Well, you'd be right. I literally walked right into the all-wood table, fracturing my shin and rendering myself completely helpless. (JK about the fracture. But you know how it is—shin and nose injuries are *no joke.*)

You'll be happy to hear that the power clicked back on before anyone needed to call 911.

I didn't tell you this story because I find it particularly riveting. I mean, it's not. I shared it because I think we can all relate to that feeling—to that tension. To be in the dark when you're meant to be in the light is an unsettling experience.

More than that, the darkness felt wrong. It created a panicked feeling and I would have given nearly anything (a piece of my shin, at least) to get my family and myself into the light again.

That's what secrets do. They shroud us. They surround our lives with a fog of unreality so dense, that it's like sitting in your house in the middle of the night in the dark. It's just not how we were meant to live.

Secrets make us *sick.* Mine made me so sick I almost *died.* Literally. But they can make us sick in other ways too. They can make us paranoid, isolated, depressed, anxious, restless, and obsessive. And secrets rarely fade into the backdrops of our lives and disappear. We'd like them to, but more often than not, our secrets have an ugly way of resurfacing over and over and over again, begging to be dealt with.

The Bible tells us as much. Luke 8:17 promises: "What is hidden will be seen. And what is out of sight will be brought into the open and made known."

Does reading that make you nervous? Is there something or someone you've shoved into the closet of your mind? A habit? A hobby? A pastime? Something you'd be embarrassed about if your neighbor or husband knew?

At seventeen years old, I had a raging eating disorder. I had an illness that touched each and every day, each and every person in my family.

I had a secret. And I was hanging on to it for dear life.

I had moved so far away from what I knew was right and good for me that it felt like I was at the bottom of the ocean, a million miles away from light or another living soul. My eating disorder made me withdraw—pushing away anyone who might get close enough to know my secret and take it from me.

It was like God's voice was calling out to me from the shoreline, a distant, faint whisper. But I allowed his truth to be swallowed by the waves, along with my health, my self-worth, and my heart.

42

FOUR

The Mean Girl

Finally, my brothers and sisters, always think about what is true.
Think about what is noble, right and pure. Think about what is
lovely and worthy of respect. If anything is excellent or worthy
of praise, think about those kinds of things.

Philippians 4:8

Whenever people hear about someone with an eating disorder, they want the details. They ask questions like, "What kind
of eating disorder did you have? Did you just starve yourself?
Or did you, you know . . ." *makes barf face with finger in
mouth.*

Look, I get it. We are fascinated with the things we don't
understand. I am no different.

Is this a good time to mention that I LOVE the show *Hoarders*?

I find myself watching the show and asking my own prob-
ing questions: *How does one accumulate 471 pig figurines, Susan?
What was inside all 700 shipping boxes in your garage? How do*

you get up to go to the bathroom? Do you get up to go to the bath-room? Where's your TV? DON'T YOU WATCH REALITY TV? (P.S. I promise I do more things in life outside of watching reality TV.)

First, I should tell you that I don't judge Susan. I know that people hear my story and say, *Um, Landra—you stuck your finger down your throat? You made yourself throw up? On purpose? More than once a day? You paid for and ate food that you knew would be in a toilet within minutes of swallowing?*

In short, yes. I did what I thought I had to do to make myself feel better. And then I did what I couldn't stop doing. Which is how compulsive behavior develops and is perpetuated—through *feelings.*

But the price I paid to *feel* better in the moment began to wear on my body. It got scary.

I remember at one point during my active addiction when my family took a trip to Florida. My brother and I went jet-skiing. (That's right, folks. I took a break from television to go into the great outdoors!) Anyway, it was over ninety degrees outside. Super warm. But I was *freezing* the whole time. I couldn't stand it, so I went inside. But no matter what I did, I couldn't get my body temperature back up.

That night, I took a bath, making the water as hot as I could handle. As I sat in that steaming water, still shivering and freezing, the gravity of my disease settled in.

Something is seriously wrong. I am sick, I remember thinking. *I am slowly killing myself.*

At the time, my family knew about my eating disorder. I had been to counseling about it and was, in their estimation, healed.

But on this trip, I couldn't hide it. They kept asking me what was wrong and I kept telling them lies.

I am not purging.

I am eating.

I am good.

I swear.

I am fine.

But I wasn't.

WHY, LANDRA, WHY?!

I asked myself that a lot.

The problem wasn't my addiction. The addiction was a symptom of the actual issue, which was my absolute inability to grasp my God-given self-worth.

I know, I know. It's super trendy to celebrate yourself. I walk through Target and want ALL THE CUTE GRAPHIC TEES. You've seen the ones I'm talking about. They have cute sayings like "Treat Yo' Self" and "Flawless" and "President of the Self-Love Club."

And I love it! I love how culture seems to be shifting toward a more positive, gentle approach to how we treat ourselves. I only wish this attitude was on trend when the story about my parents broke. Because essentially, that story triggered a downward spiral with how I viewed who I was. With how I talked to myself *about* myself.

Add my lousy self-esteem to everything else I was contending with . . . teachers at my school trashing my parents' church, being called a liar because of my eating disorder, constantly being compared to my naturally thinner twin, being placed in a special class at school due to my ADD/ADHD diagnosis, and being an athlete who never felt like I could measure up.

It felt like I was drowning in others' disappointments. And I reminded myself of that constantly.

My inner dialogue read something like this:

You're not pretty enough.

You're not good enough.

Everyone is judging you and your family.

You can't trust anyone.

You're not smart.

Something is wrong with you.

Did you know that how you talk to yourself has a significant effect on your feelings—your emotional health? It does. I once heard someone say that we have over fifty thousand conversations with ourselves a day. I believe it.

Is that my alarm? I just fell asleep! Ugh. Today's gonna suck.

Where are my fat jeans? I look awful in everything.

Why is she staring at me? What's wrong with me?

*Gosh, she's skinny. *Sucks in.* Nope. *Releases breath and digs out goldfish from purse.**

No one cares how hard I work. It's useless.

He never looks at me anymore. He probably wishes he were with someone else.

I can't afford that. I am going to be broke forever.

*These can't be my fat jeans. *Checks waistband.* Yup. I am fatter than fat now.*

Why didn't they invite me? Do they secretly not like me?

We put ourselves down countless times every day. And I am willing to bet that if we wrote down each thought on a strip of paper and placed the good, encouraging thoughts on one side of the scale, and the negative, discouraging thoughts on the other side, we'd tip the thing over in favor of the bad. And that's before we even finished with the sorting.

You might say, "I can't control what I think! After kids, I can barely control my bladder when I run up the stairs!"

But that's not necessarily the case. The Bible gives us another option.

Finally, my brothers and sisters, always think about what is true. Think about what is noble, right and pure. Think about what is lovely and worthy of respect. If anything is excellent or worthy of praise, think about those kinds of things. (Phil. 4:8)

But before we get into the specifics of this verse, we should talk about the person who wrote it.

Paul is one of my favorite people in history. Thirteen of the twenty-seven books in the New Testament have been attributed to Paul's authorship. Paul is remembered as one of the most popular apostles in the early church. His effect on the formation of the Christian community is immeasurable. In fact, Paul was the first person to put into words what being a Christ follower looks like on a day-to-day basis. So even in present-day terms, Paul's influence is pervasive and persuasive.

But Paul was also a Christian hunter. Before his transformative stroll down the road to Damascus (go read Acts 9 if you're not familiar with the story—it's a real doozy!), Paul was a religious leader who actually sought out and intensely persecuted anyone who claimed to follow Jesus and his ministry.

So raise your hand if your past mistakes, sins, and regrets serve as one of the main factors in your inability to love yourself.

Jumps up and down obnoxiously, both hands raised.

Let me ask you this: Doesn't it stand to reason that if anyone knew something about the importance of controlling their thoughts, Paul did? I mean, if you'd been Paul, wouldn't you be tempted to spend most of your thought life in the past? Thinking about how much damage you had caused to the one thing that now gave your life meaning? Wouldn't you think about all the careers, homes, and lives you had destroyed?

No? Just me?

Maybe that's one of the reasons Paul wrote this Scripture. Maybe he was speaking from experience, saying, "Think about what you're thinking about."

Yes—thoughts will pop into our heads. Ones that we don't intentionally create. But we have a choice in how we handle those thoughts. We can choose to hang on to them, rehearse them, and cling to them like a lifeline. Or we can choose to redirect them.

You can think about what is . . .

True. What does God say about you?

Pure. What are God's motives toward you?

Worthy of praise. What has God done for you to prove his faithfulness?

There's a pretty lengthy list for us to choose from. And when we move our thoughts in a different direction, we begin to hear a different voice in our head.

My daughter has the cutest, sweetest voice. (Said every mom, everywhere, about every one of her children.) The way she says *Mama* makes me want to buy her a pony pulling a truckload of toys. I could pick Sterling's voice out of a crowd of a thousand babies. I *know* her voice. I am familiar with it.

So why is it that I can't tell the difference between my voice, God's voice, and the enemy's voice in my head?

Someone once asked me, "Landra, whose voice do you hear in your head? Yours? God's? The enemy's?"

Then she talked to me about asking each thought where it came from. Sounds a little weird, maybe. But it's better than the self-deprecating alternative.

I look awful in everything.

Definitely not true, pure, or worthy of praise. So it can't be from God. And any voice besides God's has the potential to lead us down a path of destruction. And maybe none so much as our own.

During my active eating disorder, out of the 50,000 conversations I had with myself a day, 49,999.5 were negative.

The thing is, we would never, never speak to anyone else the way we speak to ourselves. We are kinder to *anyone* and *everyone* than we are to ourselves.

Maybe that's because we hear "Love yourself" a whole lot more than we hear "Be kind to yourself." Those things are similar, but they're not the same. Our parents never sat us down and said, "It's important to be kind to yourself." No, we're told how to be kind to others instead.

Loving yourself has to do with emotion. And being kind to yourself has to do with action. Which one do we have more control of? Actions, right? We can act even when we don't feel like it.

I think we could all benefit greatly from a good lesson in self-*kindness*.

Think back to your first days of school. (Some of us may have to think further back than others!) It's always kind of the same, isn't it? The teacher goes around and asks everyone to introduce themselves in some sort of creative way. (My name is Landra, so people don't usually need a way to remember that. Like, "Oh, that's *Landra*. The girl with the weird name.") Actually, the name game was always my least favorite part of the day.

"Everyone say your name and a fruit that begins with the same letter."

Why would a teacher make us do that? How is it helpful to know that there's a guy who sits three desks behind me whose name is Julio like a jalapeño? (Also, can someone confirm for me whether a jalapeño is a fruit or a vegetable? I literally just googled it and couldn't get a straight answer.)

You know what would really be helpful? If people were just honest from the start. For example, if someone were to say, "My name is Julio. Don't pick me to be your partner on a project unless you plan on doing most of the work. I am super funny and entertaining, but I definitely don't do homework."

Or, "My name is Katie. I'll be super nice to your face and even compliment your outfit. But when you're not around, I'll say some pretty degrading things about your complexion and your weight."

Or, "My name is Joshua. I am going to be the jerk of the class. Any chance I get, I'll derail the teacher, interrupt my peers, and just generally be a pain in aaallll your behinds."

Wouldn't it be easier to remember people's names that way? I'm being serious! And wouldn't it be great to know in advance the people you should avoid? You wouldn't want to sit by them, be vulnerable with them, or even cross paths with them. Think of all the time and potential heartache you'd save!

I don't like to speak in stereotypes, but there are mean girls at every school. Maybe there's a mean girl at your job or gym or in your mom group.

Imagine what it would be like if you had every single class or meeting or event with the mean girl. Imagine if you had to spend time with her every single day, side by side, just the two of you. What if you had to take a long car ride together? Sleep in the same hotel room?!

Is your anxiety level rising yet? Take it further . . .

What if this mean girl were to move next door to you? More than that, what if she had nowhere else to go in the entire world and absolutely had to move in with you? To live with you for the foreseeable future?

And just so we're clear—this mean girl makes you feel terrible about yourself. She's always making comments about what you're eating or not eating. She always points out your wrinkles and laugh lines. She is full of opinions about your job, your relationships, and your future. But her specialty is your past. She can literally recall every single mistake, awkward moment, and misstep you've ever made. And she details them for you regularly, like a broken record, over and over again.

Sounds like a nightmare, right?

Guess what? (You probably see where I am going with this, but hang with me.)

That's reality for most of us reading this right now. We live with a mean girl. We wake up with a mean girl. We go to bed with a mean girl. We are constantly confronted by a mean girl.

Let me spell it out for you.

The mean girl is you. (And me.)

Think about it. Who do you spend more time around than anyone else? Who is there with you when you get ready for the day? Eat lunch? Go to the gym? Sit in a meeting? Drive home? Go on vacation? Sleep?

It's you. Wherever you go, there you are. You can't get away from yourself, no matter how hard you try. (And trust me, I've tried.)

I am willing to bet that you've never considered just how awful you can be. Truly. I am also willing to bet you didn't know that *you* are actually the meanest girl in your life.

Have you ever listened to yourself? If someone else spoke to you the way you speak to you, how would you feel about them?

You're awkward.

You're stupid.

You're worthless.

You're ugly.

No one likes you.

I hate you.

I wish you were smarter, prettier, funnier, or just normal.

You may put your own twist on some of those sayings, but we all do it. To ourselves. Can you actually imagine keeping someone around who talks to you like that? Absolutely not!

But most of us are this tough on ourselves when it comes to our self-talk. We are our own worst critics.

It's not even something we're aware of. We don't ask Siri to remind us every other hour how inadequate we are. It's just something that happens while we're on autopilot.

If you don't read the Bible a lot, that's okay. If you're not in the habit of it, the book of Proverbs is a good place to start. It's full of wise sayings and advice on how to live. And surprisingly, even though it was written centuries ago, the words are still applicable today. You ever hear the phrase, "There's nothing new under the sun"? Well, there's really not. Our problems are not new problems. They may be a little more technologically and culturally influenced, but they have the same roots. (P.S. That phrase comes from the Bible too. Ecclesiastes 1:9!)

Anyway, Proverbs speaks to us at the very heart of our mean-girl issues: "Those who are kind benefit themselves. But mean people bring ruin on themselves" (Prov. 11:17).

Solomon is basically saying that things go well for kind people but not so much for mean people. This makes sense to us, right? Most of us can agree that we should treat others well, and when we do that, our lives are just better. There's less stress, tension, and conflict.

But for whatever reason, we never read Scripture like this and apply the same principle to our own lives. We never consider that our inability to love ourselves could potentially ruin our entire lives.

I mean, if developing an eating disorder, nearly destroying my health, jeopardizing my future, and lying to my friends and family just because I was mean to myself isn't proof of that, I don't know what is.

And we do this so often that it's rote. We don't even realize what we're doing to ourselves—we don't even realize what's at stake. We're mean to ourselves every time we . . .

eat

look in the mirror

hand in a project at work

go out with friends

try on clothes

scroll through Instagram

spend time with our family

And we don't even notice it—ever. We also don't feel like it's a big deal, because we aren't saying these things out loud. The damage is less obvious because there's no one around to yell at us or tell us that we're being cruel. But the damage is exactly the same—if not worse—than if we were saying these things to other people.

The Bible says that it's enough to *ruin* our entire lives. That may sound a bit extreme to you, but if you think about the long-term effects of what we're doing to ourselves, it seems logical.

Being mean to yourself will . . .

Cause an incredible amount of stress. When you're continually telling yourself that something is wrong with
you, it can make your brain go into overdrive. You become mentally and physically exhausted. (That's most
of us right now. Any wonder?!)

Lead you to make unwise choices. When you continually remind yourself what a screwup you are, you're more likely to act in accordance with that belief. Some of us will hurt ourselves, move from one vice to the next, or, like me, develop an addiction that only perpetuates and exacerbates the cycle. When you say awful things to yourself, you're at a much higher risk of doing awful things to yourself.

Make you completely and utterly self-focused. Let's say somehow you escape the mental and physical exhaustion, and you even avoid the poor decision-making. There is no way you're going to get out of this one. Being a mean girl to yourself will only draw your attention to one person—yourself. You'll be less likely to be others-focused and your whole balance of life will be out of whack.

This is where I got in my eating disorder. It was all-consuming. It dominated every corner of my life. Who was I going to have to lie to next? Would someone hear me purging? Would I be forced to eat something in front of someone that I couldn't keep down? I literally woke up and went to sleep thinking about me, myself, and I.

I think we can all agree on this—being mean to yourself will only hold you back.

But like a lot of scenarios, there are two sides to that coin. If being mean to yourself is *destructive*, that means being kind to yourself is *constructive*.

Think about it this way. Being kind to yourself will . . .

Give you more confidence. I don't know a single human on earth who doesn't want more confidence. I've never heard someone say, "Man, I just wish I would have walked into that situation a little less confident." No. (By the way, confidence is very different from arrogance. Confidence is a healthy self-assurance. Arrogance is something entirely different.) Everyone operates better with a little bit of confidence.

Help you treat others better. You'll treat others better because you won't constantly be looking for ways to feel better about *yourself*. You'll be able to make decisions based on what's best for other people, because you won't be so worried about what's best for you. You'll like yourself, and you won't be at the forefront of your every thought.

Give you a maturity that will influence your decisions and your life for the better. Did you know that being kind to yourself is a practice in character? It is. It takes a self-aware, self-disciplined person to show themselves grace and kindness. The more you do it, the more you build up that muscle. And the more it grows, the easier it gets. Being kind to yourself may sound like a preschool skill, but it actually takes a grown-up who understands what's at stake to practice it.

In other words, when you're kind to yourself, your life is better.

And look, this isn't about having high self-esteem. This is different from self-love and self-care. It's about more than how we talk to ourselves and think about ourselves. It's an even bigger deal than THAT. Why? We'll talk about this a few times in this book, and I hope if you get nothing else from it, you get this.

You and I were made in the image of God. THE God. The same one who created sunsets and oceans and outer space and the smell of rain. THAT ONE. We are a reflection of that God. He modeled us after himself. So what we say about ourselves reflects what we believe about God.

I am going to write that again because *I* need to hear it twice.

What we say about ourselves reflects what we believe about God.

So when you're beating up on yourself, criticizing your looks, your wiring, or your character, you are actually saying those same things about God. You're saying, "God. You did a bad job. You got it wrong with me. I actually know how to create humans better than you do."

It sounds ridiculous. But that's exactly what we do when we say mean things about ourselves.

FYI, God is not insecure. He can handle your most raw, honest thoughts and feelings. He actually wants you to bring those to him. But the problem is that when you're unkind to yourself, you're almost always telling yourself things that aren't true. They're lies. And nothing good can come from living your life based on lies. Not only can continuing to do this really screw up your sense of identity but it can also impact your relationship with others . . . and your relationship with God.

But like I said earlier, when you give yourself grace, when you affirm yourself, when you stop negative thoughts before they take root in your life and start influencing your behavior, you are actually recognizing God as a skilled and masterful Creator.

Of course, there's an obvious problem with doing all this, isn't there? Even if you really, really want to ditch the main mean girl in your life, it's not as easy as turning off a switch. I mean, we've been doing this to ourselves for so long without even realizing it. It's just ingrained in our nature. And we can have the best intentions when it comes to being kind to ourselves, but it's not a simple process.

Remember Paul? Well, he also wrote a letter to a group of Jesus followers living in the city of Colossae. He was giving them advice on how to live holy lives. And what he said to them gives us some perspective on how to deal with our inner mean girl.

Here's what he said: "But now here are the kinds of things you must also get rid of. You must get rid of anger, rage, hate and lies. Let no dirty words come out of your mouths" (Col. 3:8).

Just like the verse from Proverbs, we naturally read this passage and only think about its message in regard to other people. But Paul doesn't give any disclaimers to that effect. He doesn't say, "When it comes to others . . ." Or, "When you're talking to your friends . . ." Or, "In conversations with people you know . . ."

No. Paul says, "Stop saying this stuff. Period. End of sentence."

Anytime you say things that are angry, enraged, hateful, or not completely in line with God's truth about you, it's unscriptural. Paul tells us to get rid of things like anger and rage toward everyone—including ourselves.

I am not telling you that you can't be aware of your flaws and shortcomings. That would require a brain transplant. I mean, we all know things about our own physical appearance, skills, or behaviors that we want to change. And in some ways, it's healthy to recognize things that we need to improve on. But when that same recognition drives us to anger and rage at ourselves, it flies in the face of our God who created us for a purpose, on purpose.

One more thing about that, and hang with me for just a minute here. Don't mean-girl yourself about mean-girling yourself. Do you see what I am saying? Now that you've been made aware of it, don't beat yourself up every time you catch yourself doing it. Just acknowledge that it's happening, redirect your thoughts, and let it go.

(*Do not start singing the* Frozen *song. Do not start singing the* Frozen *song. Do not start singing the* Frozen *song.*)

You know, I actually love the way Paul puts it in the verse from Colossians. He says, "Get rid of." And the best way I know to get rid of anything is to replace it with something else. If you look back earlier in the chapter, Paul gives us an idea of what that could look like: "Think about things that are in heaven. Don't think about things that are only on earth" (Col. 3:2).

Another translation says it this way: "Set your minds on things above, not on earthly things" (Col. 3:2 NIV).

You can't control when a thought pops up, but you can absolutely decide whether it's worth "setting your mind" on all day.

Now Paul isn't just saying to think happy thoughts and tell yourself you're awesome. Paul is specific when he tells you to set your mind on "things above"—"things that are in heaven."

So instead of being consumed with you, let yourself be consumed by the One who made you. If you don't feel great, remember that God is great. If you don't feel strong, remind yourself that God is strong when you are weak. When you feel like your life is worthless, remember that God sent Jesus because you are incredibly valuable to him. The only way to stop mean-girling yourself is to take your mind *off* yourself and set it on God.

You may be surprised by how much you can like yourself. By how much you can laugh at yourself. By how much you can enjoy being *you.*

FIVE

The Thief

The thief comes only to steal and kill and destroy; I have come
that they may have life, and have it to the full.

John 10:10 NIV

Have you ever had something stolen from you? Like, straight-
up taken?

When I was dating my husband, Brad, we went to Kokomo,
Indiana, to visit his parents over Thanksgiving. And like all
the other masochists in the free world, we went Black Friday
shopping.

Now people make the assumption that because my parents
are successful financially that I probably have Kardashian-esque
carte blanche when it comes to shopping. Not the case. While
I have been afforded a wonderful, secure life with plenty of
opportunities and fabulous Christmas gifts, I am a sales-rack,
clearance-hunting, budget-making thrift shopper.

So while I joke about Black Friday, I do get excited over a
great bargain.

Brad and I joined up with our fellow psychos and we went to the mall together. And that's where I found them in all of their suede and cork-bottomed glory.

The perfect pair of winter booties.

You know the pair. The right shade. The cute toe shape. The perfect amount of heel that makes your legs look good but doesn't threaten your life each time you descend a staircase.

I snatched up those beauties with the pride of a mother holding her newborn child. I mean, obviously.

That night, we placed my baby booties with our other purchases in Brad's car. The next morning, Brad and I went to grab breakfast and we noticed the bags were missing.

We searched everywhere. And I mean *everywhere*. But they were gone. Someone had stolen them.

Disclaimer: I understand that having shopping bags taken from an unlocked car isn't that big of a deal in the grand scheme of life.

But in that moment, I felt completely violated. In a lot of ways, it was how I felt after the media coverage of my family broke out. Someone had walked over to our car, touched the door handle, smelled our air freshener, brushed against our seat cushions, and snatched the gifts we'd bought for our friends and family.

AND THEY TOOK MY PERFECT, SUEDE BOOTIES.

I was angry. I was enraged. On fire. Like a righteous indignation I felt in my bones.

I was in GO MODE. If I could have rounded up a search party of shoe-hunting volunteers, I would have. In fact, if there had been any viable recourse in finding my booties, you better believe I would have taken it. In fact, I searched for hours that day, wondering if somehow, some way I had misplaced the shoes or brought them inside without realizing it.

But, nope. They were long gone.

I know, I know. It sounds crazy. I sound crazy. But I was so mad. And this is a stretch here but go with me, please—sometimes I wish that I could get that angry about things that really matter. I wish I could get that mad at Satan when he encroaches on what's mine. Because he does. He's the king of thieves.

Here's how the Bible illustrates it: "A thief comes only to steal and kill and destroy. I have come so they may have life. I want them to have it in the fullest possible way" (John 10:10).

In the Christian world, "the thief" is understood to be the enemy—Satan. And make no mistake, he is a worthy rival. He's smart. He does his homework. He has a way of twisting the things we love and using them against us. He aims to take and take and take from us until we feel like we have nothing left.

And that's exactly what he did through my eating disorder.

I remember the first time I really knew I had a problem. I was at my grandmother's house and she had made a huge, very grandmother-appropriate spread. In other words, food heaven. I've always found so much joy around cooking, baking, and entertaining. And up until that point, eating. But that joy had been ripped from me savagely and fully.

Along with everybody else, I piled my plate high with the things carbaholics' dreams are made of. I sat down to eat like I normally would . . . only I literally couldn't do it. It felt like I had served myself tiny grenades and I was terrified that if I ate one, it would destroy me from the inside out. I was sweaty. I was nervous. It felt like everybody was watching me. Maybe they were. At that point, my seventeen-year-old frame looked like it belonged to a prepubescent child.

I pushed the mashed potatoes around, hoping they'd be hidden by the biscuit on the edge of my plate. I got up and down from the table, acting like I was grabbing a drink or a napkin. But the truth was, I was terrified. I was an anxious, nervous wreck.

Satan had taken away my ability to enjoy a meal with my family. HE HAD TAKEN AWAY MY ABILITY TO EAT A BUTTERED BISCUIT.

Why didn't I get angry? Indignant? Why didn't I fly into a rage like I had when someone had taken a pair of my shoes? This was my *joy*. My ability to feel contentment, peace, and even my ability to feel like a normal human being.

I think one reason we don't recognize the enemy's work in our lives is that we let our shame consume us. My addiction was my sidekick and my archnemesis. I loved it as much as I hated it. So I blamed myself for every consequence. And, yes, I was to blame for so much of what I was experiencing. But Satan played his part too.

He whispered, "Everybody knows something's wrong with you."

He antagonized, "You're still fat. You're still not good enough."

He shouted, "This addiction is all you have! It's the only thing you can *control*."

And I chose to believe him.

Is there something in your life that has been taken from you? Not a pair of shoes or a boyfriend but something *integral* to your well-being? Maybe it's your trust, your security, your confidence, your vulnerability, your self-respect, or your faith. All of those things had been taken from me. And I let it happen.

Did you know that in 2015, more than thirteen million Americans became victims of identity theft at a cost of fifteen billion dollars?[1]

Fifteen *billion*. I can't even imagine that kind of money. To put it in perspective, one billion dollar bills stacked one on top of the other measures 67.9 miles high.[2] Multiply that by fifteen? That's over a thousand miles of money, all taken by someone it doesn't belong to.

There are people out there who will steal *you*! Well, not really *you* (that's called kidnapping), but they'll take the *digital* you. They'll take . . .

- your name
- your social security number
- your driver's license number
- your birthday
- your address
- your bank account or credit card info
- your social media pictures
- YOUR LIFE

I am sure this list could go on and on. Information like the examples above could find its way onto a fake tax return. Or worse, the "dark web." I am sure some of you know what that is, but I don't. All I know is that I don't want to find myself or my info on something as ominous sounding as the "dark web." Ever.

People steal other people's identities for a lot of reasons, but mainly they do it for their own personal gain. (Like my suede booties, but I am *obviously* over that.) But sometimes, on occasion, they use the identities of others to provide false information to law enforcement officials.

So not only could we all wake up one day and realize that someone has run up charges on our bank accounts or credit cards, we may find ourselves with a criminal record and arrest warrants.

Now that we're all thoroughly freaked out by the reminder that we are all pretty vulnerable, let me pause here for a second and assure you that it wasn't my goal to scare you. But it is kinda scary, right? The idea that somebody can straight up steal our identities.

As most of you know, there are also people out there who make a lot of money helping people *protect* their identity. And while I am sure that these identity protection companies do a great job, I do find it odd that in order to protect our personal information from being stolen by people we don't know online, we give our personal information to people we don't know online. I mean, have you ever thought about that? I digress.

So what do we do when something valuable has been taken from us? Well, in the real world, we take immediate action. We don't wallow; we aren't paralyzed with incredulity. We get up on our feet and we *do* something. We hire someone to protect us or to get our identity back.

But that's a little ironic, isn't it? Because in the spiritual realm, when something is taken from us, we almost always do nothing. At least not right away.

See, when we think about someone stealing our identity online, we all have a clear picture of what that means. Social security numbers and bank account numbers are concrete. They're quantifiable. But when it comes to our identity in the real world, it's not quite as easy to define. Which means it's not quite as easy to protect.

A couple of months ago, I was at a Barnes & Noble (by way of Starbucks), and I heard a mom talking to her high-school-age daughter. They were huddled over a shelf of books, picking them up and reading the backs to each other. At some point, the mom shoved a book in the daughter's hand and said, "This is it! This is the book I was telling you about."

They went on to talk about the book's topic, and because I am nosy, I listened in. It was a book on discovering yourself based on your Enneagram number. The mom ended the interaction by saying, "Now is the time for you to figure out how you're wired. You've got to figure out who you are before you go to college."

I about dropped my caramel Frappuccino. If high school was the time to figure out my identity, I was a solid decade behind the game.

Can you relate? If I asked all of you to explain your identity—who you think you are and how you see yourself—to me, would it be a challenge to come up with a direct answer?

When you were young, what did you want to be when you grew up? We ask kids that all the time and I love to hear their answers. They say things like . . .

- singer
- makeup doer
- cook
- doggy doctor
- famous athlete

When I was little, I probably would have said I wanted to be either a professional basketball player or a mom. (Those identity issues start early, am I right?) And I bet if we were all honest with ourselves, we would say that we are still asking that same question. I'm sure there are some of us in our thirties, forties, and fifties who would raise our hands if someone were to ask us if we're still trying to figure out what and who we want to be when we grow up.

How many of us are still walking around wrapped up in the identity someone else gave us? Maybe a boyfriend once told us that we were too needy, so we've embraced that as our identity. Maybe a teacher told us that we learn at a slower pace than our peers, so we've embraced that as our identity. Maybe we were picked on growing up for the way we looked or how much we weighed, so we've embraced that as our identity. Or maybe we grew up in a broken home, or a home where bills never got paid on time, or a home where money was the only thing that mattered, so we've embraced *that* as our identity.

I bet there's an even bigger population of us who are still desperately trying to please our parents. We want to be who our parents want (or wanted) us to be. Or, how many of us are still trying to base our identity on the *opposite* of what our parents want us to be? Or the opposite of what our parents were?

I recently heard a talk by a man who is considered to be extremely successful by just about every conventional measure. He has been a professional baseball player and a philanthropist, has a beautiful family, and is respected by everyone in his field. He started his talk by saying, "You guys want to know what I'm struggling with right now?"

And immediately, I began filling in that blank for him.

I'm struggling with knowing where to invest my millions of dollars.

I'm struggling with deciding between which diamond bracelet to get my wife for Mother's Day.

I'm struggling with vacation destination ideas. I mean, how many times can you visit a private island off of Bora Bora before it's just mundane?

But then he said something that surprised me. He said, "I'm struggling with *approval*."

Wow. I probably sat up in my seat a little bit straighter and started to pay more attention. Because that was *not* what I expected to hear from this guy who clearly has the approval of anyone who matters. He continued to talk more, telling the audience that he continually wrestled with a deep fear that he would never be "enough" in the eyes of his dad. I think I literally leaned over to Brad and was like, "Um. He's a starter for a major league baseball team. As long as he's not out punching babies in his off-time, what else could a father want from his son?"

But it was clear this guy was still really struggling with his identity.

Because I guess making it to the absolute top of your game and being on national TV wasn't enough for his dad—or, at least, in the son's opinion. So if a professional athlete can struggle with identity issues, I guess we all can.

This probably may not come as much of a shock to you, but to resist wrapping my identity up in who my parents are and what they do for a living has been a lifelong struggle for me.

To be clear—my mom and dad never once made me feel like I needed to "behave" or "perform" a certain way because of their roles in the church. They placed no expectations on me outside of what the average parent asks from their kid.

But there is a certain amount of pressure that comes with being a pastor's kid. Especially a pastor with as much public recognition as my dad. And if you think about it, those expectations are a little absurd—are my siblings and I supposed to be genetically dispositioned to moral perfection because our parents are pastors? I wish it worked that way, but it doesn't.

So yes—the pressure to be perfect was there. (Sometimes I still feel it, if I'm being honest.)

I mean, my mom and dad are *incredible* people. Their ministry and their marriage are an inspiration to thousands—and I'm not excluded from that number. But I'd be lying if I said who my parents are didn't contribute to my eating disorder.

I remember one situation in particular. My eating disorder became public knowledge at the same time as my parents' C3 (Creative Church Culture) Conference. If you've never heard of it, the C3 Conference is a gathering of thousands of church leaders and influencers who are passionate about creating relevant and engaging environments that point people toward Jesus.

This may not sound like a big deal, but it was to me. Because I was so sick, I couldn't attend the conference, and my absence would definitely be noticed. But more than that, I wanted to be there for my mom and dad. I wanted to support them *and* support our church.

But most of all, I was worried about what people thought. I was eaten up with anxiety over it. There I was, battling a disease that was destroying my life and my relationships, and all I could think about was what people were saying about me. What they thought about Ed Young's daughter having an eating disorder.

My identity was so closely tied to who my parents were that it obscured my view of what mattered most.

And maybe you've experienced that.

I've heard people say things like this about moms of young kids: "Her entire identity is wrapped up in being a mom. It's all she thinks and talks about. I don't know what she's going to do when those kids grow up."

Honestly, I never know how to respond to that statement. Maybe it's true, but where else is she going to find her identity? (Other than in Christ, of course.) Isn't being a mother the mission and responsibility she's called to right now?

We hear this about people who have entered retirement too. They'll say it, or their kids will say it: "It's weird, now that my dad has retired, it's like he doesn't know who he is anymore."

Or when people go through a huge life event—like cancer, or divorce, or the death of a child—it's almost like their loss becomes their new identity.

I think all of this speaks into how difficult it is for us to define our identity. Because we're not talking about numbers and accounts and dates—we're talking about intangible factors that are complex and in flux. So if it's hard for us to even *talk* about our identities in specifics, how are we supposed to know if our identities are grounded in the right things?

Like a lot of things in life, when we don't know where to find answers to our questions (often questions we don't even know we're asking), we'll simply let other people answer them for us.

More about that in a minute. First, let me say that finding answers to the question, "Who am I?" is *super* important. It's foundational to what this book is about, because how can you love someone you don't even really know? How can you celebrate the triumphs of someone if you don't know how far they've come?

Maybe even more than that, knowing who you are is key in order to make nearly every decision that comes our way. Because it's important to make choices that protect the critical pieces of our identity.

I know this is a little heavy—like, Landra, isn't it time for a *Bachelor* reference?—but don't turn off your brains just yet! Because if we really get this right, it can not only help us figure out who we are but it will also help us figure out who we're *not* supposed to be. In fact, I believe that learning about our identity has the power to change the way we feel about ourselves more than anything else we can do.

And if we're not careful, we'll fall victim to all kinds of identity theft.

Okay. Remember earlier when I was talking about the GO MODE I got into when I realized I'd been robbed? You've probably experienced a similar reaction if you've ever been stolen from or had part of your digital identity compromised. You launched into GO MODE and immediately started calling credit card companies and banks.

Spiritually speaking, we can do the same thing. When our confidence is rocked, we can take immediate action. When our trust is shattered, we can take immediate action. When our self-respect is destroyed, we can take immediate action. When anyone or anything tries to steal our identity, we can and should DO something.

Instead, we—myself included—often do the opposite. When we feel insecure, disappointed, rejected, or hurt, we freeze. We feel like we can't move. We get stuck in emotional quicksand that seems to suck us lower and lower into states of depression or resentment.

But the Bible tells us that when something is stolen from us, we can do something about it. Like, right away. Listen to this promise from 1 Peter 5:

Be watchful and control yourselves. Your enemy the devil is like a roaring lion. He prowls around looking for someone to swallow up. Stand up to him. Remain strong in what you believe. You know that you are not alone in your suffering. The family of believers throughout the world is going through the same thing.

God always gives you all the grace you need. So you will only have to suffer for a little while. Then God himself will build you up again. He will make you strong and steady. (vv. 8–10)

Peter starts off with a warning—one much like the one I just gave you.

The devil is a jerk. He's sneaky and greedy and he's on the hunt. His prey? *You.* Your children. Your spouse. Your friends. All of God's people. We should never underestimate our enemy.

But do you see that fourth sentence? Do you hear what Peter's saying?

Stand up to him.

Say that out loud. *Stand up to him.* Get a good neck roll going when you say it next time. *Stand up to him.* Work a mean finger snap and put on your best I-am-bad-and-I-know-it face and say it like you mean it.

STAND UP TO HIM.

That's the first step. Tell the enemy he *can't* take your joy, your trust, your confidence, your self-love. Tell him you serve a big and mighty God who has already crushed him beneath his heel and you will *not* be a victim to his garbage drama *one more second.*

Not everyone has to experience regret before they learn a lesson. Or maybe you're already there, and that's why you're holding this book. If that's you, it's not too late. You can stand up to the enemy. But if that's not you, and you're fresh off a loss and still reeling, you can stop the spiral right now before it takes you any further. You can stand up to the enemy.

The next step? Remain strong in what you believe.

Belief is different from feeling. Belief is something that happens in the head and the heart. Belief relies on faith. Belief relies on what you've seen happen in the past to others and to yourself.

You believe that your plane will safely get you where you need to go because you've flown many other times.

You can also believe that God will give you what you need when you need it because, in the history of the world, he's never let us down.

Remain strong in what you believe. When I am struggling to have faith, I like to make a list of all the times God has come through for me.

God gave me loving parents.

God made a way for me to get the help I needed.

God sent me a loving husband.

You'll have a list of your own. Prayers God answered. Prayers God *didn't* answer. Prayers others prayed for you. Examples from your walk with the Lord and examples of prayers answered in the lives of people around you. Celebrating what God has already done is the best way to bolster your belief.

God did it before. He brought you out of that situation, that relationship, that job, that dark place, that debt—he will *do it again*.

Finally, and this is one thing that we often forget: "You know that you are not alone in your suffering" (1 Pet. 5:9).

I felt so incredibly *alone* in my suffering. I can literally remember thinking:

No one knows what this is like.
No one's been in my shoes.
No one's ever felt this way.
No one's messed up like this.

The enemy would like nothing more than for us to feel like lone soldiers, stranded by ourselves on the battlefield of life. But the Bible dispels that myth. Peter writes, "The family of believers throughout the world is going through the same thing" (1 Pet. 5:9).

The context of that Scripture passage is Peter encouraging the younger members of the early church. But he was telling them exactly what I am telling you—with God, you can get through anything.

You've heard that before. Maybe so often that you've become numb to the miraculous power of its truth. But think about *everything* the early church overcame.

false teachings (James 2:1–3)
corruption among leaders (James 2:14–26)
misunderstandings regarding faith (James 3:1–4:12)
gossip (James 5:13–20)
persecution (1 Pet. 1:1–9)

You see that those listening to Peter's words were feeling a lot of the same emotions we do. Anxiety, confusion, betrayal, victimization.

Peter basically said, "Hey, you're not alone in your pain. Other people have hurt and are still hurting, just like you. And not only are other people experiencing the same thoughts and the same hurts, but Jesus himself has endured deep emotional and physical wounds on your behalf. He knows what you're feeling too" (Isa. 53:3–4, my paraphrase). Sweet friend. You. Are. Not. Alone. In. Your. Pain.

Just let those words wash over your raw heart. Let them be a balm to you. *You are not alone.* Any thought otherwise is a lie from the pit of hell and you should call it out as such.

Peter also said,

God always gives you all the grace you need. So you will only have to suffer for a little while. Then God himself will build you up again. He will make you strong and steady. (1 Pet. 5:10)

What a promise. God *always* gives you the grace you need. God himself will build you up again.

Raise your hand if you're really good at having to learn lessons the hard way. *Raises both hands.*

Yeah, I am with you. See, as a pastor's kid and a lover of Jesus, I heard these truths over and over again growing up.

I believed the enemy's lies too long. I even made his job easier by creating lies of my own. Lies that would very soon be exposed, stripping me of every relationship and every comfort I held close.

SIX

Tell Me Lies

Those who trust in themselves are fools.

Proverbs 28:26 NIV

Have you ever been to a magic show? Or watched on TV as an illusionist does one of those crazy tricks where it appears like they've made an eighteen-wheeler disappear in the middle of the desert?

It's insane, right? Logically, we know what they're doing isn't possible. We know there's some sleight of hand, hidden compartments, and mirrors involved. But to the human eye, it all looks completely legitimate.

But it's just an optical illusion—our brains creating a visual trick of their own. Even though we *know* what we're experiencing is fake, our minds struggle to believe what our eyes don't see.

Ever heard of any of these?

The Spotlight Effect
The Barnum Effect

Heuristics

The Halo Effect

Hindsight Bias

Change Blindness

False Memories

These are all examples of ways our minds play tricks on us. They influence us without our awareness and sometimes convince us of things that aren't even true.

Why am I bringing this up? To demonstrate that our minds aren't always the most reliable source when it comes to knowing what's real versus what's an illusion.

Proverbs 28:26 puts it fairly straightforward: "Those who trust in themselves are foolish."

I mean, tell us how you really feel, Solomon.

But he makes a point.

When we operate based solely on our own thoughts, feelings, and opinions, we are putting our trust in ourselves. And sometimes—let's be honest—"ourselves" are not the most trustworthy source. That's because we have a very limited perspective of what is actually true. Without relying on the wisdom of the Bible and the experience of others, we're like travelers trying to navigate uncharted territory and only working with a portion of the map.

And more often than not, when we put our trust solely in our own capabilities, we wind up making choices that we regret.

One of my biggest regrets has always been how often I misled my parents during my eating disorder. When I was about eighteen years old, my addiction to bingeing and purging was running rampant. It controlled me, like a leash around my neck, jerking me wherever it wanted to go. And I truly believed that what I was doing was okay because I was protecting myself and protecting them from the truth that would potentially hurt us all.

My parents had long since realized I had a problem and connected me with a local therapist. In our sessions, I told more half-truths and lies to convince her of what I was trying to convince everyone else.

I am okay. I am fine!

And in the distorted, strange recesses of my mind, would you believe that I deceived myself? I tricked my own mind into thinking that I had the disorder under control. But like we spoke about in chapter 3, what's in the dark will almost always be brought into the light, one way or another.

Have I mentioned that my parents are incredible? Not just as parents but as human beings as well. They've never made my siblings or me feel judged or pressured or like we had to be perfect to uphold anyone's perception of our family.

Every reason I hid my eating disorder had to do with *me*—my wrong way of thinking. The lies I had convinced myself of.

But because they're incredible people and parents, they were highly invested in my recovery.

Outside of therapy, I told everyone I was cured; that I'd had a *breakthrough*. I told them I was eating without purging, maintaining a healthy exercise regimen, and even feeling good about myself again. So when my parents asked to sit in on one of my therapy sessions, I freaked out.

I tried to go in before them and prep my therapist. I don't know what I thought I would say . . . *Hey, so. I know I am still really sick, but can we pretend for the next half hour that I am not?!*

Whatever manipulation I had planned never got the chance to take place, because we all went into my therapist's office together.

And that's when the lights came up on all my darkness. And not just a pleasant dinnertime glow. We're talking about a 4 a.m., flashlight-in-your-eyeballs level, stark, glaring light.

"I am sorry," my therapist said to my parents. "Landra is not doing great. She's not even doing well. In fact, I can't treat her anymore. She's at such a severe weight, it's my recommendation she be admitted to an inpatient facility immediately."

That's when I heard the words I had been running from since the moment I started bingeing and purging. "Landra, you need to go to rehab."

I recently saw part of a Netflix documentary called *Amy* on the late singer-songwriter Amy Winehouse, directed by Asif Kapadia.

What I saw *moved* me.

The film opens with a breathtaking fourteen-year-old Amy, already rocking the black eyeliner and bellowing with a gritty, raw voice that was far older than its owner. One thing that stood out to me was the absolute *focus* she had. The command of her performance. The clarity of her gaze.

But at some point over the next couple decades, Amy's focus, command, and clarity dissolved as she battled with addiction. Struggles with bulimia, drugs, and alcohol ravaged her frame and her spirit. And, ultimately, those same struggles took her life on July 23, 2011.

I remember one particular moment in the segment when some people in Amy's inner circle approached her about rehab. They told her that her father was fully on board with the course of action, so she loosely agreed to go. But on one condition— her father had to tell her to her face that he wanted her there.

So they took Amy to her father and, unfortunately, he buckled under her ultimatum. He couldn't tell her that she had to go to rehab.

And look—I get it. My daughter, Sterling, is just a toddler, but she's already mastered the art of getting what she wants. I can't imagine having to look her in the eye and tell her she needs to go to inpatient treatment because she has a severe mental health issue. I can't say I would have done anything different, so this is not an indictment of him or his parenting.

But don't you think he wishes he had said go? Not just *go* but *run*! Run as fast as you possibly can, Amy. Go and stay until you're well.

Sometimes the best thing we can do for someone else is to hurt them.

And thank God my parents were willing to hurt me.

To say I was averse to the idea of going to an inpatient treatment facility would be like saying I am averse to the idea of being held up at gunpoint. The idea made me want to crawl into a deep dark pit and never come out again.

But I was given no other option.

The entire mood of my situation shifted. It was go time as far as my parents were concerned. The research was done to find the best place to send me. They looked in Dallas, Chicago, and all over the United States. Phone calls were made, doors were shut, and conversations were had. Sometimes I was involved in those, sometimes I wasn't. I had lost the right to control my own life and for good reason. I was hurting myself. I was killing myself.

I wish I could tell you that it was *then* that I had an *aha* moment where I decided to make healthy choices for myself. I wish I could tell you that my addict behavior ended in light of all the pain and chaos it had caused both me and my family.

But still, I couldn't bring myself to truly embrace the gravity of my malnutrition. I had a long phone interview with the admissions office of the treatment facility my parents finally chose. During that call, the admissions consultant asked me about my eating habits, how often I binged and purged, how much I weighed.

And I lied. I lied, knowing that there was no longer a reason to lie. I lied because that's what we do when we're so used to hiding and stuffing; it feels like first nature. I told myself I was protecting myself, but the truth is, I was lying because that had become my pattern.

The appointment with my therapist had been on a Thursday. By Sunday, I was landing in the great state of Arizona for inpatient treatment for an eating disorder.

Between the time that I was told I had to go to rehab and boarding a plane to get there, I called each of my siblings and told them where I was going. Each one reacted in kindness—accepting, loving, and encouraging me. But still, I couldn't tell them how bad it was. I downplayed it. I avoided the explicit truth, even when I literally had nothing else to lose.

The truth is, everyone lies. We lie to ourselves constantly. We lie to others constantly. Mostly, we tell little white lies. We lie to cover up mistakes. We lie to cover others' mistakes. We lie for a hundred different reasons.

But the most harmful lies we tell are the ones that are useless. That have no payoff. Think about it—when we lie for no reason, all we're doing is lessening our own integrity. We're degrading our own character. We're ripping at our own moral fiber.

The Bible mentions lying and liars several times. On many of those occasions, it's referring to the enemy—to Satan—as the king of liars. I don't know about you, but any practice that puts me in the same category as the devil is one I want to avoid.

Along with sharing one of Satan's most prominent characteristics, the Bible has the following to say about liars.

In Proverbs 6:17, a "lying tongue" is listed among the seven things the Lord hates.

In Proverbs 12:22, "lying lips" are called an abomination to the Lord (NIV).

Proverbs 19:9 warns that a liar will not go unpunished.

Psalm 101:7 says that no one who lies and cheats will live in the Lord's house.

In Colossians 3:9, Paul tells the early church to stop lying to one another. He says lying is how they lived before knowing Christ, and it has no place in their new life.

I really tried to think of and find some milder verses on lying, but these *were* on the tamer side. The Lord *hates* lies. They're an abomination—something that causes disgust or hate. Lies won't go unpunished. Liars won't live in God's house because lying to one another is what people who don't know Jesus do.

Aren't you thankful for the grace of God right now? I sure am. In hindsight, I do feel flashes of guilt and condemnation for the lies I told. But the blood of Jesus covers those now. Hallelujah!

It breaks my heart to think about how sick I must have been to not share my truth with the people who love me unconditionally.

Rehab. It wasn't a place I foresaw myself going. Ever. I was covered in shame.

How did I become someone who needs rehab? I wondered. But isn't that a little ridiculous? Isn't that like someone drowning in the ocean, flailing their arms and begging for help, being embarrassed when someone throws them a life vest?

Why do you think it's so hard for us to ask for help? When our kids ask for our help, do we shame them? Do we whisper about them to our spouses when they're not in the room? Do we even *hesitate*?

No.

I think as we grow older, we expect ourselves to have it together. When we were kids, we envisioned ourselves as adults knowing exactly what to do in any given situation. But when we get to the age of "adulthood"—whatever age that is—we suddenly feel like impostors. Like everyone around us seems to navigate their problems and issues with ease while we still feel like our thirteen-year-old selves, conflict-avoidant and insecure.

Culture doesn't help. You can't get online without seeing a new "Boss Babe" or "Mom-Blogger" who curates their home beautifully, grows and purees their own organic baby food, and wears actual grown-up makeup. Every. Single. Day.

Life is good at making us feel like we're the only ones.

The only ones who cry in the bathtub for no good reason.

The only ones who feel exhausted by 3:00 p.m. and crave bedtime as if it were oxygen.

The only ones who don't have time for a decent social life, much less time for self-care.

The only ones who have regrets.

The only ones who don't measure up.

If the enemy had his way, we'd all feel like the only people on earth who needed help.

I think the main reason I didn't want to ask for help was that, in many ways, I wanted to stay sick. As much as I hated my body and hated the way my disorder had taken over my life, the cycle that I had gotten caught up in was my constant—my control. *Mine.*

I knew that once I spoke out about it, I would not have control of it anymore. Each tiny bit of my secret that I shared felt like I was handing over my power—my control—bit by bit. And God? Sure. I would say over and over how I wanted God to be in control of my life. But that was another lie. I wanted control. And not just a little. I wanted all of it.

I also wanted to stay skinny. I mean, I'll be honest. I was afraid that if I ever got help and started eating again, that I would gain an exorbitant amount of weight and hate myself even *more.* To me, the only route to happiness was to stay sick, stay thin, and protect my secret through whatever means possible.

Outside of not wanting to let go of my secret, it was also difficult for me to ask for help because I was afraid. Maybe you can relate to that. I was afraid of every possible outcome. I was afraid I would be . . .

rejected
exposed
told I am too far gone to be helped
made to feel less-than or weak

Why do we do that? Why do we always assume the negative what-ifs are more likely than the positive what-ifs? Because isn't it just as possible that I would . . .

be accepted

find grace

be seen and known and loved anyway

get *better*

But for some reason, when it comes to our problems, we often don't see the possible benefits of putting ourselves "out there" because we're too focused on the possible pitfalls.

Another big reason people don't ask for help is pride. I can't say that was my particular issue with my eating disorder, but I've definitely let my ego get in the way of asking for help in other instances.

We're afraid we'll be seen as weak. But isn't asking for help the opposite of weak? Think about it.

What takes more courage, speaking out or staying silent?

What takes more bravery, taking a step or remaining still?

What takes more strength, being comfortable or making progress?

But did you know that asking for help is honoring to God? It is.

God created us with a need for help. It's part of his design for us as humans.

Even in the garden of Eden, God set it up so that Adam required provision and help rather than being able to do everything on his own. From a sustenance standpoint, God gave Adam food, water, even companionship through his own presence. But then God realized that Adam needed something else—or some*one* else. So he said, "It is not good for the man to be alone. I will make a helper suitable for him" (Gen. 2:18 NIV).

Do you see that? God even called Eve Adam's *helper*. Part of Eve's purpose was rooted in humanity's need for *help*.

Not a *friend*.

Not a *partner*.

Not a *lover*.

A helper.

You don't have to be a Bible scholar to study God's Word. In fact, you don't have to be any kind of scholar. If you've got Google, you've got a pretty powerful tool at your fingertips.

In fact, Google is exactly how I learned that the word *helper* in Genesis 2:18 is the Hebrew word *ezer*.[1]

It's used many times throughout the Old Testament as someone who comes alongside anyone who needs any kind of help—people helping their neighbors or relatives (Isa. 41:6), people helping in a political alliance (Ezra 10:15), and military reinforcements (2 Sam. 8:5).[2] *Ezer* is also used in reference to God as a helper sixteen times, so this word describes a very powerful kind of help and rescue.

So when we deny ourselves our own needs—our own humanity—it flies in the face of the God who created us to be vulnerable, communal, and yes—needy!

Even before sin came into the world, God's design was for us to need help and to give help to one another. In other words, God foresaw Adam needing all sorts of help, so he created Eve to meet those needs.

Another way asking for help is honoring to God is that it's actually helpful to other people—it's a service to *them* in many ways.

In our mind, we've believed the lie that asking for help would make us a burden to others.

I don't want to drag them down.

I don't want to be draining.

I don't want someone to have to carry this weight for me.

But do you know what the Bible says about that?

"Carry one another's heavy loads. If you do, you will fulfill the law of Christ" (Gal. 6:2).

Crazy, right? Not only is needing and giving help part of how we were created but it's also part of what Christ requires of us who love him. Not surprisingly, the Bible stands in direct contrast to the lies we've chosen to believe about asking for help.

We actually allow others to fulfill the law of Christ when we invite them into our hurt, our pain, and our suffering.

First Corinthians 12:12 says, "There is one body, but many parts. But many parts make up one body."

Where we are weak, God made it so that we can lean into others' strengths. When we're honest enough to ask for help, we give people the opportunity to operate out of their God-given gifts and talents.

One last way asking for help honors God is probably the most important. When we ask for help, we acknowledge that we can't go through life on our own, and that we stand in need of a Savior.

Asking for help is not the equivalent of failure. But make no mistake—we do fail. According to Romans, "Everyone has sinned. No one measures up to God's glory" (3:23).

See that first word? *Everyone.*

Those Boss Babes? They've failed.

Those Mom-Bloggers? They've failed.

That girl at work with good hair? She's failed.

Everyone has and will continue to fail.

Even pastors. Even pastors' kids. (Some would say *especially* pastors' kids!)

But somehow, over time, we convince ourselves that we should not fail—that we should never have a reason to ask for help. But then God will show us, sometimes gently, sometimes with what feels like a huge push, that we are wrong in that thinking.

As Paul points out, God said, "My grace is sufficient for you, for my power is made perfect in weakness" (2 Cor. 12:9 NIV).

God tells us that his power is perfected when we are weak because that's when he's the strongest.

In our heads, we know these things. But in practice, the lies we've *believed* become louder than what we *know* to be true.

Maybe it's a strange thought to you—that God *wants* us to need him. But he does. He wants us to recognize that his grace is the difference-maker in our lives. And when we ask for help—from him or from others—we are doing just that.

So, no, when I was a little girl, I didn't think, *When I grow up, I want to go to rehab*. No. No. No. It was a nightmare in every sense of the word. And let's be honest—it's not like I was even *asking* for help. Going was an act of submission, not an act of bravery. But I went.

To rehab.

Alone. I had never left home by myself before.

I was on a one-way flight to a state I had never been to before—to a facility I never imagined I'd need.

SEVEN

Hope Is the Thing with Feathers

Hope deferred makes the heart sick.

Proverbs 13:12 NIV

Hope. It's such a pretty word, right? And a pretty name.

What about *faith*? I am not a huge "words" person, but these are two of my favorites.

But let me ask you this—what's the difference between having hope and having faith? Because faith and hope are not the same thing.

Sure, "Have faith" and "Have hope" have the same general connotation. Like, just believe that something good or better is about to happen, right? Yes, we use the words interchangeably, but if you break them down, they have different meanings and different functions in our lives and in our walks with God.

Hope *feels* good, doesn't it? Poet Emily Dickinson said that "'hope' is the thing with feathers / That perches in the soul."[1]

First, don't be impressed. English and poetry were not my strengths in school. I totally googled that. But isn't it true? Having hope fills your chest with anticipation and expectation. So much so that sometimes hope can make it feel like your heart could take flight at any moment.

On the other hand, when our hopes are never realized (at least in the way we want them to be), it can feel like a death in some ways. The Bible supports that: "Hope that is put off makes one sick at heart" (Prov. 13:12).

That's a perfect description, isn't it?

When we get dumped, don't get the job, receive bad news at the doctor's office, lose a friendship, or feel rejected, it can all just make our hearts feel sick.

So if that's you right now—I feel you. I've been there. And the Bible says it makes *sense* to feel that way. But, like I've said, feelings are temporary. Sometimes it's just nice to hear that someone else has been there and been through it.

Jerome Groopman, author of *The Anatomy of Hope*, talks about the science of hope and its effect on the human body.

> Researchers are learning that a change in mind-set has the power to alter neurochemistry. Belief and expectation—the key elements of hope—can block pain by releasing the brain's endorphins and enkephalins, mimicking the effects of morphine.[2]

Okay. Well, that's amazing. Thanks, God, for making the human body such an incredible and miraculous thing! But there's more! Groopman goes on to say, "In some cases, hope can also have important effects on fundamental physiological processes like respiration, circulation, and motor function."[3]

In other words, hope heals. Literally. It doesn't just make you *think* things are better, it scientifically *creates* a better reality for your mind and your body.

I can honestly say that the entire time that I struggled with my eating disorder, I always had this little, tiny speck of hope. Hope that one day I could eat like a normal person. Hope that one day I would be well again. Hope that one day I would stop lying to everyone I loved. I had hope that one day I would not harbor such genuine dislike for myself and my body.

I had hope.

It wasn't a big hope. It wasn't grand and sweeping. And if my hope was a feather, it would have been one single really straggly looking one that had been plucked nearly clean.

But I had hope all the same.

The thing about hope is that it's a lot like being vulnerable. It takes a bit of courage to have hope. I mean, how many times have you said, "I am not getting my hopes up," because you didn't want to be disappointed?

But let me ask you this. How many times have you starved your mind and body of expectancy by refusing to have hope?

Hope can be life-giving. But in my case, it was life*saving*. Because it was enough to leave the door to recovery open—if only just a tiny crack.

But it's still hard, isn't it? How can we have hope when we've been let down so many times? How can we have hope when we're tired? How can we have hope when we've seen so many other people struggle and not get the answer they wanted?

In 2008, Duane Bidwell, an associate professor of practical theology at Claremont School of Theology in California, conducted a study on hope among kids with chronic illnesses.[4] He, along with his colleague Dr. Donald Batisky, studied tons of data from a diverse group of children who all shared an end-stage kidney failure diagnosis.

(Pause while I go squeeze my daughter. Sick kids get me, y'all.)

Anyway, after analyzing the results of their study, the two doctors defined five steps to healthy, hopeful living called the "pathways to hope."

1. **Maintaining Identity** by continuing to participate in activities and relationships that help patients retain a sense of self outside diagnosis and treatment.
2. **Realizing Community** through formal and informal connections that help patients understand they are not alone in living with disease. This community is made real through conversation, visitation, consultation, and participation in daily activities.
3. **Claiming Power** by taking an active role in treatment by setting goals, self-advocating, monitoring, and maintaining one's own health.
4. **Attending to Spirituality**, activated through religious, spiritual, and other contemplative practices.
5. **Developing Wisdom**, which involves both gaining pragmatic, medical wisdom derived from one's own experience and finding ways to "give back."[5]

Okay. Yes, these are medically geared pathways, but if you think about it, they can still apply to us when we're in need of hope.

1. **Maintaining Identity.** When we're feeling hopeless, don't we tend to withdraw? Don't we tend to wallow in our heartsickness and obsess over things we can't control? Anybody? Just me?!

   One pathway to hope is maintaining (or reinforcing) identity. In other words, remember who you are. We do that best by getting outside of our pain.

   Go to the gym. Bake your favorite casserole. Pick an old hobby back up. No, you're not going to *want* to do these things. That's not the point. Or maybe it is the point.

   One of my favorite quotes is often attributed to Albert Einstein. He supposedly said, "The definition of insanity is doing the same thing over and over and expecting different results."

   Like, obviously. But we do this all the time! (And by *we* I mean *me*. Surely I am not alone in that!) We do the same things over and over again. Then we're disappointed over and over again.

   We have to do something different if we want something different to happen.

   The point is that you have to remember that you are more than the sum of your current circumstances. You are more than your bad choices. You are more than your addiction. You are more than your rejection. You are *more*. And honestly, who you are has way less to do with *you* and way more to do with *who made you*.

   You are *more*—so get up and remember who you are.

2. **Realizing Community.** This is no shocker, right? We need community. But here's the thing. We need a *specific*

type of community if we want to create or sustain hope through our pain. We need at least one other person who is going through what we're going through, or who has *been* through what we're going through.

I know that, for me, it can be difficult to make new friends. Wasn't it so much easier when we were kids? You wait in line for the slide together on the playground and all of a sudden, you're besties. In the adult world, my life is pretty structured. I go to the same places, do the same things, and see the same people. There isn't much built-in opportunity to create new relationships.

I get that. I am there. But this is so important. We have to push ourselves to get in a community group, sign up for that fitness class, or invite an acquaintance to coffee. It will be worth it, I promise!

3. **Claiming Power.** Don't you just love this one? It makes me want to put on a bodysuit and crank some Beyoncé! (Only, I haven't lain out in the sun since Sterling was born, and I am pretty sure the sight of my pasty legs would literally blind people. So as a service to the general public, this scenario will stay strictly fantastical.)

So how does one "claim power" as a pathway to hope? In the research example, the kids took an "active role in treatment by setting goals, self-advocating, monitoring, and maintaining one's own health." I mean, what if we all just started there and threw the rest of this book out the window? (Please don't throw my book out the window.)

Goal-setting doesn't have to include a vision board and a weekend retreat in the mountains. It can be as simple as:

- make your bed in the morning
- take a walk after dinner
- skip Starbucks twice this week and put the money in a jar

Goals give us short-term hope.

Now let's talk about self-advocating. This is something that I am not great at. At all. I think it's difficult for those of us who struggle with our sense of self-worth. But we do this—whether or not we realize it. During my active addiction, I fought for my secret. The secret that was destroying me and my relationships. How messed up is that?

Let me ask you this. What are you fighting for right now? Are you fighting for a relationship that is not good for you? For a promotion that would ultimately distract you from your family and loved ones? For a number on the scale?

If what you're fighting for doesn't get at the very heart of God's best for you, you're probably (definitely) advocating for the wrong thing.

Here's one last way to claim your power. Monitor and maintain your health. Look, I am not about to lecture y'all about your health. You have mamas and doctors for that. But your health should never be a back-burner subject. Your personal health is the only health that you have total control of. Your health affects every breath you draw, step you take, and decision you make. And it also plays a role in your ability to have *hope*.

4. **Attending to Spirituality.** Isn't it great that this is a scientifically proven pathway to hope? First of all, I am assuming you're reading this book because you have a desire to grow spiritually. (Or because you know my dad and he somehow talked you into reading this as a personal favor to him.) Either way, if you want to spark hope, you have to look to the One who created the notion in the first place. Feeding your spirit is just as important as the nourishment you get from feeding your body. Your soul needs attention to survive.

   Prayer, meditation, church, worship music, walks in nature, friendships with people who have a faith you crave—these are all integral steps toward hope.

5. **Developing Wisdom.** Again, I find it so fitting that the idea of getting outside of one's own self is listed in a medical research analysis. You can't get away from God, right? He will reveal himself everywhere, regardless of the context.

   Here's the thing about the way we were designed. We're a lot like flashlights, designed to shine our lights outward. If you shine a flashlight in your own face, it's blinding (not to mention painful). You can't see anything besides your own light. But when you flip that sucker around and shine it away from you? It's like magic. The darkness is pierced. What you couldn't see suddenly comes into view.

   It's the same with our lives. When we live a life that's me-centric—where all we do is think about ourselves (which often plays out as worrying about what other people are thinking about us)—we're not functioning the way we were made to function.

It's only when we shine the light of our lives on others that we are living out God's will and purpose for our lives. And our ability to have hope springs a few new feathers.

So let's review. Why did we even start talking about hope in the first place?

Because we need hope to get by. We need hope to take care of ourselves. Even the tiniest shard of hope is worth fighting for. It's worth choosing one of those pathways today and doing whatever it takes to *work* on having hope.

Because it was that one, feeble little shard of hope that took flight and carried me into rehab. Rehab was just a stop on my journey, but hope ended up being that straggly, feathered thing that saved my life.

EIGHT

Have a Little Faith

He replied, "Because your faith is much too small. What I'm about to tell you is true. If you have faith as small as a mustard seed, it is enough. You can say to this mountain, 'Move from here to there.' And it will move. Nothing will be impossible for you."

Matthew 17:20–21

Remember how I said there's a difference between faith and hope? There is. And we're going to get to that. But before we get there . . . it's been a minute since we've visited with *The Bachelor*, hasn't it?

Did you know that there are entire websites devoted to "*Bachelor*-isms"—words and phrases that are said so often on the show that they've been added to its lexicon? Here are some of my favorites.

"I think we are really starting to have a connection."

"I've never felt like this before."

"I think I am really starting to fall in love with him/her."

"This is so much harder than I thought it would be."

"He/she really opened up tonight."

"I just thought we had something real."

"I could leave here with a ring on my finger!"

"I've got some really tough decisions in front of me."

"I've been hurt in the past, you know? It's really hard for me to open up."

"What does he/she have that I don't?"

"I never thought I would feel this way about someone this fast."

"I am really taking a leap of faith by being here."[1]

We've heard that last one before, right?

I am taking a leap of faith.

What exactly does that mean? The answer to that question highlights the difference between hope and faith.

Hope has more to do with our *will*. Our *dreams*. Our *goals*.

Faith has more to do with our *walk*. Our *demeanor*. Our *actions*.

Hope and faith are tied; they're difficult to separate. The Bible says, "For we through the Spirit wait for the hope of righteousness by faith" (Gal. 5:5 KJV).

We use our faith to wait for the hope of righteousness.

Another verse differentiates faith and hope this way: "Now faith is confidence in what we hope for and assurance about what we do not see" (Heb. 11:1 NIV).

Even there, faith is depicted as just a shade more committed than hope. It's a subtle difference—but a difference all the same.

I haven't been super specific about my experience in rehab, and there's a good reason for it. I want to be very clear—seeking inpatient treatment was the best and only choice I had at the time. If you're considering inpatient treatment of any sort, I would encourage you wholeheartedly to get the help, support, and tools that you need.

I am so thankful for my experience there because it contributed to my journey to restoration. At the same time, coming home from rehab was not the experience I thought it would be. In fact, what happened next was the opposite of what everyone expected. I got sicker.

And again—to reiterate—my condition worsened because I wasn't prepared to do the work to get well.

When I was discharged from rehab, I remember getting on the plane in Phoenix to fly back home. I felt strange—out of sorts. My self-confidence was at an all-time low. It was like I wasn't even inside my own body anymore.

On the plane, some guy was trying to talk to me, and instead of engaging like I normally would, I pretended to be asleep. It was like I had shut down some integral part of myself—the outgoing, bubbly girl who was confident enough to strike up a friendly conversation with a stranger.

When my parents picked me up, I'm sure they fully expected to pick up the healthy, happy girl they knew prior to my eating disorder. But that's not who I was. I was withdrawn, depressed, and unsure of what was ahead for me.

During treatment, I had no contact with the outside world apart from phone calls with my parents. When I was released, I entered outpatient treatment where I went to therapy every single day. Afterward, I would come home and zone out completely.

It was almost like I regressed emotionally—I didn't want my phone, I didn't want to watch TV. I spent most of my time alone, coloring in coloring books and worrying about my future.

Rehab was an important step. It showed that I was willing to let someone inside my secret with me. It took away the "safety" I had felt in hiding. But once my secret was exposed, it was like I was paralyzed with shame and doubt.

Like my parents, I thought that treatment would "cure" me. That it would be like a magic wand had been waved over my life and everything would go back to "normal." But that didn't happen. I needed to do more. I needed to follow up my step of hope with acts of faith. Faith that God could bring light to the dark places in my heart. Faith that I was lovable, despite my brokenness.

And that's true for most of the challenges we face in life. Hope on its own can carry us a long, long way. But hope without action—without *faith*—will eventually wane. Hope requires faith for fuel.

And like hope, it doesn't take a lot of faith to make a difference. In the often-quoted Scripture, we hear Jesus say:

> Because your faith is much too small. What I'm about to tell you is true. If you have faith as small as a mustard seed, it is enough. You can say to this mountain, "Move from here to there." And it will move. Nothing will be impossible for you. (Matt. 17:20–21)

If you have a pen or pencil handy, go ahead and underline the first word of the last sentence. Write it in the margin of this book. Say it out loud.

What will be impossible for those with even the tiniest bit of faith?

Nothing. Nothing will be impossible for you.

Look, I don't know what mountain you're standing at the bottom of. Maybe it's divorce. Maybe it's infertility. Maybe it's job loss, financial hardship, or an addiction of your own that you're battling with. We all have mountains that we have to face. (Sometimes it can feel like we're the only ones with major issues, but trust me—God doesn't skip anyone on the mountain-handing-out.)

What I do know is that nothing is impossible for those who have faith (hope + action)—even if their faith is as small as a grain or a mustard seed.

My first act of faith was going out west to rehab. It didn't heal me. There was no immediate result. But it was something.

Maybe your act of faith is making an appointment with a counselor. Or telling a trusted friend the thoughts you're having. Or joining a gym. Or cutting up your credit card.

Whatever it is, regardless of how big or small, our acts of faith carve pathways for God's miracles in our lives. But once we make steps, we can't stop. We have to keep moving if we want to get to the other side of our mountain.

Okay, so check this out. Several times throughout the Bible, Jesus tells people that their faith was the difference-maker in their journey. In the Gospels alone, there are ten examples of Jesus performing a miracle based on the faith of the healed, saying, "Your faith has healed you."[2]

And then look at the beginning of Mark 6. Jesus is teaching in his hometown of Nazareth and is rejected by many of his own people. As a result, his ministry there was not as noteworthy as it had been in previous areas. Verses 5 and 6 tell us this: "Jesus placed his hands on a few sick people and healed them. But he could not do any other miracles there. He was amazed because they had no faith."

My first reaction to this passage of Scripture is to be absolutely appalled by the faith of the Nazarenes. Because it was their *lack of faith* that hindered Jesus's miracle-working. But when I really think about it, I feel a sense of embarrassment. Because I wonder how many times my lack of faith has limited God's movement in my moments of need.

When we demonstrate faith, when we take a step toward Jesus with an action, discipline, or practice, we are setting the stage for life change that can only take place through the grace and power of our heavenly Father.

Demonstrating faith requires something of us. It requires action. It also requires courage. For a lot of people, that presents a very important question: Is it worth it?

For me, that question comes up a lot. Especially when there's a menu involved. One of my favorite places to eat is a West Coast burger chain called In-N-Out Burger. It's a little slice of heaven on a plastic tray. In fact, they even print a Bible verse on each of their cups. So obviously it's God's will that I help myself to as much of their food as possible whenever I get the chance.

But really, there are few things better in life than a double-double burger with fries from In-N-Out Burger. It's my all-time favorite. (Thank GOD for recovery food, am I right?)

The problem is, after I eat it, I don't feel amazing at all. In fact, I feel sluggish, tired, and honestly a little ill.

Now this has *nothing* to do with the quality of In-N-Out Burger. It has everything to do with the speed at which I inhale their food. And that, for the sake of my husband and child, I normally try to prepare and consume healthy meals. So my body isn't used to all the delicious grease and spike in caloric intake.

But it never fails. Even though I can predict the physical outcome, I still can't force myself to make better eating decisions when it comes to In-N-Out Burger. In the moment, it just seems so worth it.

Can you relate? Have you ever found yourself trying to decide if something was worth it or not?

Maybe you . . .

Have a huge project due at work, but The Final Rose episode is airing and you can't decide if it's worth it to blow off your responsibilities and indulge your raging curiosity.

Know that hanging out with a certain group of friends brings out qualities in you that you aren't exactly proud of, and you can't decide if it's worth it to protect your integrity and stay home alone or to go out.

Committed to an exercise plan, but it's taking a lot more effort than you anticipated. You can't decide if it's *really* worth it to prioritize your health over your current discomfort.

Decided on some physical boundaries with someone you're seeing, but it seems like they're losing interest. You can't decide if maintaining those guardrails is worth the possibility of getting dumped or cheated on.

I don't know you, but I do know this—we each face a ton of decisions every day. And let's be real, we usually know what the *right* choice is. At least, deep down we do. But the issue is that knowing the right choice and making the right choice are two different things. Knowing the right choice doesn't always mean it's easy to *make* the right choice.

That's because the real question is this: Is making the right choice worth it or not? Whether it's at the burger counter, the gym, the office, or in the privacy of our own homes, it's a question we all ask.

And it applies to our faith more than any place else. To some degree or another, we've all looked at the whole church and God thing and wondered, *Is this going to be worth it?*

Maybe for you that question comes up when you consider what God says about your habits, what you prioritize in life, or what you do with your body. And sure, you know that God is *technically* right about those things. I mean, he *is* God. But you wonder if it's going to be *worth it* to do what he says.

Or maybe it's not what he's *said* that worries you, but what he *might say* if you chose to follow him wholeheartedly. Will he say that you have to quit doing and saying things that you love? Will he say that you have to dress a certain way or like certain kinds of music? Will he say that you have to sell all your stuff and change your focus? The truth is, a lot of people who choose to follow Jesus lead different lives than they would without him.

First of all, I want you to know that it's okay to ask these questions. If you wonder if it's all worth it, that doesn't make you a bad Christian or a bad person. It makes you a human being.

In fact, some of Jesus's best friends and closest followers found themselves facing the very same question. One was a guy named Matthew. Matthew seemed to have it all together, but in reality, he was living in two separate worlds. He was a Jewish guy, yet he also worked as a tax collector for the Romans.

In that culture, tax collectors were thought to be the worst of the worst. (I mean, not much has changed in that regard, but back then, it was on a whole other level.) The Jewish people resented tax collectors because they took their money for taxes (and then added a little bonus for themselves). Tax collectors were seen as traitors and thieves who exploited their own people for selfish gain.

On the other hand, people were still willing to be tax collectors even though they were hated. Why? It had its benefits. They made a lot of money, so even though people didn't like them, it gave them the resources to make sure they were taken care of financially (plus, it gave them some protection within the Roman government). So in that regard, life wasn't too bad as a tax collector.

Matthew was in the middle between the good and the ugly. Maybe you can relate to that dynamic. It can't be an easy one to navigate. But one day, Matthew had an encounter with Jesus that changed everything.

Jesus was just finishing up a few miracles.

As Jesus went on from there, he saw a man named Matthew. He was sitting at the tax collector's booth. "Follow me," Jesus told him. Matthew got up and followed him. (Matt. 9:9)

In case you zoned out for a moment, Matthew just got up and started following Jesus. No questions asked. He simply stood up from the table and walked away.

But here's what's crazy. The table held everything that provided for him. It was his tax collector's booth. Following Jesus meant walking away from his livelihood—one that made him a lot of money.

Sure, Matthew probably had a little background on Jesus. He knew Jesus was a teacher. He had probably heard about Jesus's miracles and how Jesus offered hope to broken people. But to get up and walk away from his life? Matthew *had* to have asked himself—either in that moment or later—"Is this really worth it?"

And here's something I don't want you to miss—we don't know a lot about Matthew's story. In fact, we read a majority of it in this verse. But we do know this: Matthew didn't get his questions answered before he moved. He had *no clue* if it was going to be worth it. Jesus didn't spend the next three days explaining to Matthew what would happen (or not happen) if Matthew followed him.

Jesus simply said, "Follow me," and Matthew had to decide to take a leap of faith and say "I'm in," even though there was no guarantee of what would happen next.

In that moment, Matthew decided to trust that Jesus had far greater things planned for him than what was on his table. And honestly, that initial step made all the difference in his life. There were tough moments for sure. Matthew gave up a lot for a life of adventure and unknown by following Jesus.

But I think if Matthew were here today, he'd tell you—with no question or hesitation—that it was totally worth it. Why do I think that? The book of Acts tells us that after Jesus was crucified and came back to visit his friends, he then ascended into heaven, and the apostles returned to Jerusalem.

When they arrived, they went upstairs to the room where they were staying. Those present were Peter, John, James and Andrew; Philip and Thomas, Bartholomew and Matthew; James son of Alphaeus and Simon the Zealot, and Judas son of James. (Acts 1:13 NIV)

Did you catch that? Right in the middle of the list of Jesus's followers, there's Matthew's name. After Jesus was crucified, Matthew may have had the opportunity to quit, pack it up, and go back home—maybe even back to his old life as a tax collector. Yet, he didn't. Long after Jesus went back to be with his heavenly Father, Matthew was still "in." Just like his first step away from his tax collector's booth, Matthew continued to take steps toward following Jesus.

But it all led to a life that Matthew *never* would've traded to go back to the table. I believe Matthew would tell us that showing great faith, great big beautiful faith, is always worth it.

And hey, when you try to decide if all of this is really worth it, God's not mad at you. He's not nervous, uncomfortable, or hurt. He knows that it takes courage to step into the unknown. He's not asking you to have it all figured out. He just wants you to get started. To start following him by taking a step. Just one step toward him.

Don't be like I was for so long. Don't let your fears or your doubts stop you. They aren't deal breakers. Even in the midst of them, you can still take a step away from the table. Trust me, I know how hard a step that is. Because there's always something on the table—something that seems better in the moment. Something that seems more predictable, alluring, and attractive.

But you will never know what God will do unless you take a step.

Whatever it is that is holding you back, you don't have to conquer it overnight. You just need to know this: Following Jesus starts with a step. For you that might mean . . .

Taking the first step. For some of you, it's time to give this Jesus thing a *real* chance. You've heard enough about him. Maybe you even grew up going to church. But somewhere along the way, you've hesitated, and you just need to muster up the courage to jump in and start putting the things that you've heard into practice.

Taking the next step. Maybe you've already made a decision to follow Jesus, but it hasn't really changed your life—at least not in a way that would be noticeable. Maybe your next step is to carve out some time to get to know him better. To commit to reading the Bible on a regular basis or praying at the same time each day. Or maybe your next step is to be more like him by beginning to serve others in the way that Jesus served.

Taking a step back. There have been *so* many times when I've been consistently doing things that have caused a roadblock in my relationship with God. If you can relate, your next step might be to say no next time. To your boyfriend or girlfriend. To that second glass of wine. To that late-night scroll through Instagram. To the girls' night invitation that always leads to you feeling worse about yourself and your life. You may need

to get someone you trust involved for accountability—
someone to help you say no.

Over and over again, people find that committing their lives
to Jesus begins with one step toward God and toward growing
their faith.

Your personal faith matters. Not just for your own benefit
but also for the benefit of others.

Did you know that there are countless times in the Bible
where *someone else's* faith was the difference-maker in a person's
life? Someone's mother, brother, or friend had enough faith in
the healing power of Jesus that it was enough to help them,
regardless of where their own faith was.

The faith of the centurion saved his servant in Matthew
8:5–10.

Jairus's faith helped his daughter receive healing in Mark
5:35–43.

Jesus healed the paralytic man because his four friends had
such great faith in Mark 2:3–5.

There are many other examples of this "transference" of
faith. Jesus did and does work through the faith of others.

I don't know many people whose faith has been tested as
many times as my parents', yet I've never seen them waver—
not even once. That's not to say that they've not had prayers
go unanswered. They have. We all have.

But unfortunately for my parents, many of their trials have
been very, very public.

But there is one issue in particular that hits especially close
to my mama-heart. At six months old, my brother was diag-
nosed with a genetic disorder of the nervous system called

neurofibromatosis. This disease affects how nerve cells grow and form. Basically, tumors grow all over your insides. Neurofibromatosis can lead to a lower life expectancy, learning disabilities, as well as hyperactivity disorder. As a mother, I can't imagine how it must have felt to receive this news. And about a *six-month-old*. How out of control must that have felt? How unfair?

But my mom never wavered in her positivity and faith. (I mean, I'm not saying that's what we *all* should do—I'm just saying that was what she did.) Instead of freaking out and shutting down, my mom and dad accepted the diagnosis and used it as one more way they could honor God with their steadfast trust.

Now that's also not to say that they've never been angry with God. They have been. And God's okay with that. But their faith is the stuff of concrete confidence.

And I truly believe that their faith was one of the immeasurable factors in my recovery. Their faith and the faith of those who prayed for me for countless hours on countless occasions.

So I want you to think about something. Take a moment to think about how the faith of others has saved you. It's humbling, right? Now think about this. Do you have people you're actively demonstrating faith for?

Sometimes acts of faith can feel a lot like standing naked in front of a room of strangers. You're cold and you're vulnerable and you feel like you are all alone. That's how I felt when I boarded the plane to Arizona. It was the first time I'd left my family, my secret was exposed, and I didn't know if I'd ever see home again. But I took that step all the same.

NINE

Label Maker

Do not fear, for I have redeemed you; I have summoned you by name; you are mine.

Isaiah 43:1 NIV

Do you follow any of these Instagrammers who style their fridges? Like, the ones who get all these cute, clear bins from The Container Store and color coordinate their juice boxes so they appear in rainbow order? It's amazing. I am genuinely amazed.

As someone who loves to entertain (and someone who has a toddler who is forever in desperate need of a snack), I am constantly opening and shutting my fridge. And you know—it has never once struck me that I could organize my produce by texture and display it in a crystal dish. I am really not making fun of the practice—I love looking at those organized fridges!

These bloggers also style their pantries. I mean, have you seen these works of art? They've got every nutritional bar available in perfect stacks in a trendy, Pottery Barn basket. I am pretty sure Sterling would take one look at that basket and take its cleanliness as a personal challenge to her seek-and-destroy skills. But my *favorite* part? THE LABELS.

Did anybody else have one of those huge, clunky label makers that punched letters into different colors of tape? Talk about a throwback. I loved my label maker. I labeled aaallll the things.

- Landra's Hairdryer
- Landra's iPod
- Landra's Makeup Bag
- Landra's Notebook
- Landra's Room (You know, in case someone got lost in my house and needed reassurances as to where they were.)

What about you? Do you label your stuff? Your kids' stuff? Are you a Sharpie-on-the-tag kind of labeler? Or do you use a machine?

Here's the thing about labels. We like them because they help us organize things, places, and people into categories. They especially apply to people—we each wear all kinds of labels—physically and metaphorically.

For example, I'll never forget the time my brother called me fat. I was young, like thirteen. And I was nowhere in the vicinity of being overweight. He's going to read this and feel terrible, but he should not. Everybody's brother calls them fat at some point. (It doesn't make it okay, but it's a fact.) I called my brother all kinds of names, and I am sure he never internalized a single one. But for some reason, that insult stuck with me. It became a label I wore for the next decade.

Some of the metaphorical labels that we wear are unavoidable. For me, these include:

- preacher's kid
- Brad's wife
- twin
- baker
- friend
- Sterling's mama
- pastor

These are things that I am just *known* for. They're inextricably related to who I am and what makes up my nature.

Think about the labels you wear. How did you write your bio on Instagram or Facebook? If you're like me, you probably spent more time on it than you're willing to admit. I mean, how do you summarize your whole life in a few words? Did you talk about the sports or musical instruments you play? Your dog? Your family? Your collection of Happy Meal toys from third grade?

How exactly do you explain who you are to somebody else in a couple of sentences?

Have you ever been somewhere new with people you don't know, and someone asks you to wear one of those "Hello. My Name Is _____" stickers? The reason people want you to wear the sticker is to let everyone else know who you are. And that's great—people knowing your name is powerful. But you should also know that there's so much more to who you are than your name, right? Your name is what people call you. But your identity, the real you, is something else entirely.

But who is the real you?

That's a strange question, but it's actually a very important one. Because who you are, and who you *think* you are, will dictate a lot about your life. It'll impact . . .

> **Who you hang out with.** Almost all of us choose to hang out with people we think are like us. So who you think you are in some ways determines your friends.
>
> **What decisions you make.** Will you work hard, be loyal, be generous, read your Bible regularly, or maybe even run for president? So many of your choices will be based on the categories you put yourself in.
>
> **How you treat your body.** What you think about you will influence your approach to things like alcohol, exercise, drugs, etc.
>
> **How you treat others.** What you think about yourself— good or bad—will influence how you treat other people. People who view themselves in a healthy way typically treat others well. The opposite is true as well.

Point blank: your view of yourself affects the quality of your present and future.

And here's what's crazy. Even though most of us don't know who we are, we still get tons of messages each day that are trying to fill in the blank for us. Without realizing it, many of us identify ourselves with labels—labels that were given to us by other people.

We get messages from our spouses, bosses, coworkers, parents, friends, and people we don't even know on social media. Not to mention the billions of dollars spent each year on ads trying to convince us of who we are or should be (only, of course, if we buy their product). It seems like everywhere we look, there's some type of message about who we are, who we're not, and who we should be. Not only do the negative messages outweigh the positive but we usually remember them longer. Without realizing it, we are collecting messages that somehow form our identity.

These collected messages become who we think we are.

Can you remember a time in the past when someone said something negative or hurtful to you about who you are, and now—months or even years later—it has shaped the way you think about yourself? (Sort of like when my brother called me fat.)

Maybe a teacher told you you'd never succeed.

An ex told you that you were needy.

An investor told you to chase a new dream.

A friend told you that you were selfish.

A pastor told you that your action was unforgiveable.

We don't know how to fill in the blanks about who we are, so we let other people fill in the blanks for us. When they talk, we listen.

And this is totally normal. Because you and I don't have a lot of available time on our calendars each day to figure out who we are. And it doesn't help that who we are, to a certain degree, is in flux. We're always growing and changing. And we're busy. We're worried about what's for dinner, whether we'll get the promotion we've been working so hard for, whether our spouse is happy, and what the doctor is going to say when they call.

Sitting down and figuring out who we *are* at any given moment is not on top of our priority list. I totally get it.

However, if we understand how much the answer to that question impacts our lives, we might spend more time thinking about the answer. Who *you* think you are will impact nearly every other decision you make. It certainly did for me.

So you and I have work to do, right? If we want to embrace who we are, we have to figure out who we are. We have to figure out which labels can stay and which labels need to go. In order to do that, it's important that we test and question the labels that have been placed on us—the messages we're repeating to ourselves about ourselves. And we have to decide who has the right to give input into our identity and who doesn't.

You know what's coming next, right? God has something to say about who we are. In fact, God has *everything* to say about who we are. But right now, let's just look at part of what he says.

It comes from a letter in the New Testament that was written by one of Jesus's friends. John was one of the famous twelve disciples and was most likely one of the youngest of the group when he started following Jesus. He also lived the longest.

In the first several years following Jesus's death and resurrection, when Christianity was illegal, the other disciples were nearly all killed for their faith. But somehow John managed to stay alive, making it to old age (although he was exiled and put in jail, at least he was alive).

It's generally believed that when John wrote this letter, he was in his last years on earth. He probably knew that he was one of the oldest people alive who had actually walked and talked with Jesus. (Gosh, can you imagine?) John knew that his time on this side of eternity was drawing to a close, and he had limited time to relate any last details he thought were important to the remaining followers of Jesus. So what did he choose to talk about?

He talked about what God thinks is true about you and about me. Here's what John wrote:

> See what amazing love the Father has given us! Because of it, we are called children of God. And that's what we really are! The world doesn't know us because it didn't know him. (1 John 3:1)

First of all, how beautiful are the words of God? I mean, come on!

Okay. Let's break this down. John tells us that God is *crazy* about us. He loves us an *amazing* amount. We'd be awestruck if we ever allowed the truth of God's love to really sink in. Another translation of the same verse says that God "lavished" his love on us (NIV). It's like an overflow of amazing love, almost unseemly in its incredible amount and depth.

For those of us who struggle with self-love, if you only take one thing away from this book, let it be that God loves you . . . and not only that, he *likes* you. He thinks you're funny. He thinks you're cute. He thinks you're brilliant. He wants to hang out with you. (That's actually in the Bible—check out James 4:8.)

What God thinks about you may not feel as *urgent* as what others think of you, but it is the ultimate deciding factor in your worth.

But there's one other thing that makes what God thinks about you a big deal. And it's this—unlike your coworkers, friends, spouse, and Instagram marketers, even unlike your close friends and family—God knows who you really are. God knows what your labels are. The good, the bad, the ugly. He knows the *real* you.

Thousands of years before John wrote that letter, God spoke to a kid named Jeremiah—a kid who, like many of us, didn't necessarily have stellar self-esteem. And God said, "Before I formed you in your mother's body I chose you. Before you were born I set you apart to serve me" (Jer. 1:5).

Have you ever thought about what we are before we are born? Souls? Angels? Dust? Glitter?! It's a strange thought but, according to the Bible, we're something. And God looked at Jeremiah, just like he looks at you and me, and he said, *That one. I want that one. The world needs that one.*

He formed you in your mother's body—on purpose and for a purpose.

So the first label you can put on yourself reads as follows: *Chosen by God.*

You should write that down somewhere you can see it every day. Write it on your hand. Write it on your mirror in dry-erase marker. Write it on a notecard and stick it on your fridge. *Write it on your heart.*

You were hand-selected by the Creator of the universe.

If you look through Scripture, you'll see that God said similar things to other people. And they were all people he knew very well. Why? Because he created them—he chose them.

I mean, think about it. If you're a parent, who knows your kids better than you do? Who can decipher their unintelligible babble better? Who knows how they like their grilled cheese better? Who knows where to find their cutest freckles and scars? Us—their earthly creators.

Think about how much more God knows us. No one knows us better than the One who created us. And no one should be able to place labels on us but him.

Back to our first verse from John's first letter. When John wrote that God loves you, that's a message that should have the most influence on how you feel about yourself. That label should have the ultimate veto power over all the others. Why? Because God actually knows you—*the real you*—better than anyone else. And that's why what John said next makes so much sense. "The world doesn't know us because it didn't know him" (1 John 3:1).

John is saying that culture—the media and the ones putting labels on us—doesn't always see the whole picture. They don't know God, so they aren't good judges of his children. That's not to say that there aren't Christians functioning in the mainstream media. But I think we can all agree that God's opinion of us is rarely (if ever) factored in to what's marketed to us and the messages our culture relates to us.

God is still the best judge of what labels you should be wearing. Even your closest friends and family cannot be good judges of the real you. For one, they didn't make you. And maybe just as important—they don't even know who *they* are. All the times you've been told that you *are* something you don't want to be, or *aren't* something you do want to be, remember that those messages came from people who are still trying to figure out who they are too.

Think of it this way. Have you ever seen one of those "All About Mom" handouts that parents post online? They're these sheets that teachers help kids fill out about their parents, filling in the blanks with whatever the kid says.

They usually say some pretty amazing stuff. Like, "My mom is thirteen years old. She likes to eat macaroni for dinner. Her favorite hobby is playing with me and drinking mommy juice."

And to the kid, all the information is completely accurate. Because they see the world through a biased perspective, just like everyone else. People can't see us clearly because they can't see *anyone* or *anything* else clearly. That includes us and how we view other people and how we view ourselves.

And that's true of your identity too. If you want to know who you are and who you should be, you can't rely on the people around you, because their perspective is biased and always changing.

God, on the other hand, is constant. He isn't trying to sell you anything. He doesn't need anything from you. He doesn't need you to succeed or fail in order to feel better about himself. He doesn't have a perspective problem. His view of you is based on his creation of you, which is undeniably true.

When I left rehab, I put monster-sized labels on myself, including,

- addict
- broken
- unfixable

Even the label that I was someone who had gone to rehab was difficult for me to come to terms with. At the time, I didn't realize that getting help is actually the bravest decision someone can make when they're unwell.

I wish I had been better about embracing God's thoughts toward me. I had had God's truth spoken over me my entire life, and even during my eating disorder, I would have told you I believed them. But I didn't live like I did. My negative self-talk certainly didn't reflect those beliefs. I didn't treat myself like I believed one word of what God said about me.

Other people aren't the only ones mislabeling us. We can be the worst perpetrators of sticking negative labels on ourselves. Some of my self-appointed labels include:

- overweight
- irredeemable
- not enough
- unintelligent
- unlovable
- needy
- liar

But here's the tricky part about these labels. At some point, they all, at least in part, felt very true. So they stuck to me. And I was too sick, too scared, too broken to rip off those labels and tear them to shreds.

But it's hard, right? How can we sort through all our labels and only keep the ones that are true? Earlier I talked about how most of us have heard negative comments that have, in some ways, shaped how we view ourselves.

Let me ask you this. What would it look like for you to allow what God says about you to shape you in the same way?

What if you started filling in your blanks with God's words and not yours and others'?

Instead of sick, needy, and unlovable, what if it were loved, chosen, and worthy?

You can't stop people from having a commentary on who you are. You also can't force the world around you to stop advertising products designed to convince you that there's something wrong with you that needs fixing. You'll never be able to control how often or how loudly the messages come in about you.

But you *can* give those other voices some competition. You can consistently remind yourself what God thinks about you. You can stay so connected to God that his voice is louder than anyone else's. And you can surround yourself with friends who will repeat what's true about you over and over.

And that's exactly what saved me.

TEN

Shame-Sick

God so loved the world that he gave his one and only Son. Anyone who believes in him will not die but will have eternal life.

John 3:16

I wish this was the part of the book where I said I exited rehab and never got sick again.

Like I've already said, my experience in treatment, while certainly a leap of faith, was not as successful as it could have been because of my own inability to accept God's truth. Because I was believing lies and accepting labels from everyone *but* God. I hear stories all the time about people who enter rehab programs and find the courage to truly seek healing. And although I had a little bit of hope that I *could* recover, I was not willing to make the long-term commitment of genuine recovery at that time.

You may need to make several acts of faith and take many steps toward healing before your recovery begins too.

Here's the truth—and I'm ashamed to admit this even now—I was so sick, the only things I took away from my time in rehab were new methods to keep my addiction alive and well. I can actually remember lying to people about why I was in the treatment center to begin with. I think I told some of the other patients that I was there for depression or anxiety or something. I mean, if you're willing to lie to an addict about your own addiction, you are still in a seriously bad mental spot.

Honestly, when I sat down to write this book, I had to really think hard to remember one clear image from my time there. I think I blocked most of it out, it was so traumatic. The issue was that I could meditate for hours, meet with a hundred counselors, have calories forced into my body all day and all night, but I still would have been sick. Because my disease had infected every area of my body—especially my heart.

If I had to choose a word to describe my heart condition when I checked out, it would be *shame-sick*—deeply embroiled with guilt and embarrassment.

Have you ever heard of this new Instagram phenomenon of dogshaming? It's one of those social media trends where people post photographs of their dogs with signs describing all the bad stuff the dogs did.

You should really pause here and give yourself a few minutes to investigate the trend. It's hilarious. I just opened Instagram and searched under #dogshaming. Here are some of the best results.

"I shoplifted from Pet Smart."

"I bark at men to keep Mom single."

"Celebrated my 3rd birthday by pooping on the rug."

"I ate a bottle of glitter and now my poop sparkles."

"I snuck into my brother's (pig) litter box and ate all the 'chocolate.'"

I mean, I could easily get lost in the tempting Instagram time vortex of reading and looking at these puppies. Some of the dogs have multiple postings and have garnered a little bit of a following. They're shame-famous.

My favorite part of all the pictures is how happy some of the dogs look. They're grinning from ear to ear, with no clue whatsoever that their owners are completely selling out their most embarrassing moments. It's amazing.

But how glad are you that this trend does not apply to our human failures? If it did, I am pretty sure I would end up being one of the shamed who got quite a following because I would have so much fail-material to pull from.

Maybe you feel the same way. Maybe some of your signs would say things such as:

"Did something at a party that I regret."

"Said something I totally should not have."

"Was really mean to my kids."

"Didn't get the promotion."

"Can't sleep due to anxiety."

Wow. Our failures aren't nearly as funny or cute as the dogs' signs, right?

The truth is, no matter what our signs would say, we've all got major failures that we don't want to publicize. For me, the highlights would read something like this:

"Anorexic *and* bulimic."

"Lied to everyone who loves me—again and again."

"Terrified to get pregnant because I don't want to gain weight."

"OCD and controlling."

"Consistently overcommitted."

"Lose patience with my toddler regularly."

Yeah. Definitely not the kind of things I want people posting about me. And yet . . . I rehearse these lines to myself over and over again. Are you the same way? Do you constantly self-shame?

When you and I get caught up in rehashing all the bad things we've done and numbering all the ways we've let other people down, we begin to believe that we are actually *bad*. That's what's at the heart of shame—the belief that there is something intrinsically bad or wrong with us. And shame—shame is a powerful, powerful liar. It has the power to just *linger*—to creep up as a constant reminder of all the ways we don't measure up. After a while, we start believing that we are worthless, we're losers, we don't have much to offer, and anything good we do is only an exception to who we really are at our core.

Here's what we do. We make promises to ourselves to get better, to *do* better, convinced doing so will make us better—will redeem us and make us good somehow. For me, I told myself that I would "get better" soon. I told myself that I would come up with a diet plan or an exercise plan that would keep me thin, but allow me to stop lying to my family and friends. Then I would try it . . . and I would fail.

Then I would try again . . . and I would fail.

Again.

And again.

And again.

The cycle was *brutal*.

And the self-shame would take on increasing levels of ugly.

When we've messed up or feel like we don't measure up, shame shows up in a couple of ways.

The first is anger. We get frustrated because other people seem to be doing great, but we're not. We get mad at ourselves, and assume that God is mad at us too. And ultimately, we want to quit trying.

We also experience shame through our sadness. We feel depressed because it seems like no matter how hard we try, it's never going to get better. We're never going to be able to stop doing whatever it is we're doing (or start whatever it is we want to start), so why even bother?

Sometimes it's both. It's overwhelming and defeating and we just want to quit.

You want to know when this cycle is especially toxic? When it's especially debilitating? When it comes to our relationship with our heavenly Father. It's one thing to feel like we've let ourselves down. That stinks. It's another thing to feel like we've let the people we care about down. That's awful. But to feel like we've let God down . . . that's almost unbearable.

But let me ask you this: Do you think that's how God wants it to be? Do you think he wants your relationship with him to be your biggest source of shame?

One of the things we as Christians believe is that if we want to know what God is like, we should study the character of

Jesus. Because he was and is our best source to know what God thinks or would do and say in any given situation. That's difficult for us to do sometimes, right? Like I said earlier in the book, we can't put ourselves in God's shoes because we're not God. The way he gives, forgives, and loves is unlike anything we're capable of. Because we're not him.

So if we want to get to know him, if we want to try and assume we know what he's thinking about us, we have to study his Son.

John 3:16 is one of the (maybe *the*) most frequently quoted verses in the Bible. Maybe it's the first Scripture verse you memorized. It was definitely one of mine. And I am willing to bet that it's been printed on billboards, signs, and T-shirts, and tattooed on bodies probably more times than we can count.

But have you ever read John 3:16 in context? Do you even know why Jesus said what he said? Check this out:

> Now there was a Pharisee named Nicodemus. He was one of the Jewish rulers. He came to Jesus at night and said, "Rabbi, we know that you are a teacher who has come from God. We know that God is with you. If he weren't, you couldn't do the signs you are doing." (John 3:1–2)

If you know anything about Nicodemus, you know that he was kind of a big deal. He was a religious leader during Jesus's time on earth, and the leaders had it in for Jesus. A lot of people think that's why he came to see Jesus under the cover of night, when no one could see him. Nicodemus was a lot like us—he was worried what people would think of him.

He didn't want it getting out that he was someone who spent time with Jesus.

Nicodemus started off their conversation by acknowledging that Jesus was from God and not the monster the Pharisees were making him out to be. And isn't it just like Jesus to cut right to the quick of what Nicodemus was really after? He didn't engage in a long monologue, defending himself or reprimanding Nicodemus for being on the "wrong" side of the argument; he simply told Nicodemus how he could have a personal relationship with the Father.

And, no—none of us have to sneak around to meet with Jesus. But if you're anything like me, you've wondered (sometimes desperately) what you have to do or say (or not do or say) to be "in" with the Father. In other words, how *good* is *good enough* when it comes to God?

Because this culture followed Jewish law, being "good" with God meant following over six hundred rules. Now if you're a rule follower like I am, doesn't that sound like living in the middle of a land mine? I can't imagine how the people back then could ever feel like they were "in" with God. And I also bet there was a ton of self-shaming going on. Maybe that's what prompted Nicodemus to go see Jesus in the first place.

Here's what Jesus said in response to Nicodemus's unasked question:

> "What I am about to tell you is true. No one can see God's kingdom unless they are born again."
>
> "How can someone be born when they are old?" Nicodemus asked. "They can't go back inside their mother! They can't be born a second time!" (John 3:3–4)

Jesus and Nicodemus went back and forth like this, Jesus trying to explain what it means to be born again, and Nicodemus grappling to understand the concept. Finally, Jesus broke it down for him very simply. And that's where our famous Scripture comes from.

In John 3:16, Jesus said, "God so loved the world." We've all heard that before. In fact, we've all probably heard it so many times that we have become numb to it. But for the Jews living during this time period, that statement would have been groundbreaking. Nicodemus probably tilted his head or gasped or something.

I am sure he snuck away to see Jesus expecting to get the new rule book. Expecting to get a new to-do list he could check off because he wanted to be "good" with God.

And man oh man—can I relate. I have struggled with (and sometimes still do) walking around with a sense of shame because it feels like no matter how hard I try, I can't check all the boxes. I can't get everything done. I can't measure up.

Can I get an amen?

Maybe you think that when God looks at you, all he sees is your drinking, your impatience with your kids, your messed-up family history, the sexual mistakes you've made, the habit you can't quite break, or the envy you have for those with "more." Maybe you think that when God thinks about you, he thinks the same thoughts you do. I did. I kept telling myself how disappointed God had to be with me. There I was, an incredibly loved girl who was born into this amazing, fun, kind, and blessed family, and I was harboring a huge, nasty secret. And I was trading in the respect and trust of those I love just to keep that huge, nasty secret. How could God think anything good about me? I hated myself. Surely he hated me too.

But Jesus said it to Nicodemus, just like he says it to you and to me. It's what I said in the last chapter, but it goes a step further. Before anything else, you are *loved*. Unconditionally. Not when you are *good*. Not when you *obey*. Not when you *follow the rules*. Out of the gate, for free, 100 percent of the time—*you are loved*.

We're like that as parents, right? The moment our kids are born, when we hold them in our arms for the first time—before they do anything right or anything wrong—we love them all the way.

And that's just the beginning. Jesus finished his statement with these words: "God so loved the world that he gave his one and only Son. Anyone who believes in him will not die but will have eternal life" (John 3:16).

Brad and I are pretty romantic. Read: we make people nauseated. We *love* love—especially the precious love we share for one another. We have so many songs between the two of us—from "Tennessee Whiskey" by Chris Stapleton to Frank Sinatra's "The Way You Look Tonight." Sometimes words are just words until you put the right music behind them. Then they're magic.

One song we love that illustrates my point here is a classic—Bryan Adams's "(Everything I Do) I Do It for You." You should look up the lyrics! But even the title speaks to the heart of the song. I love you, so I'm going to do something for you. Isn't that the kind of love we all dream about? No one dreams about the kind of love that is expressed through *words* alone. We dream about the kind of love that drives someone into action. A love that someone is willing to die to prove and protect.

That is the exact kind of love God has offered to each and every one of us. He doesn't love us because we're good or bad. He loves us because we're his. And because his love for us is so deep, wide, and pure, it cannot be contained by words alone. It moved our Creator into action—because he could not stand to be separated from us.

So he gave his Son to pay a huge price so that we never have to.

I can imagine Nicodemus's response: *I don't have to follow six hundred rules? I don't have to be perfect? I don't have to do one thing to be in with God?*

I pray right now that God allows you and me to have the same awestruck wonder at his great love for us. It is incredible.

Again, there's more to the story than *just* John 3:16. I mean, that would be enough, but Jesus kept talking. Here's what he said next: "God did not send his Son into the world to judge the world. He sent his Son to save the world through him" (John 3:17).

Think about it.

God loved you before you did anything right or wrong.

God loves you right where you are in this moment, right now.

God made the *ultimate* sacrifice so that you could have a relationship with him.

But there is no part of your relationship with God that was created for condemnation. There is no part of your relationship with God that should bring you any amount of shame.

Because Jesus didn't come to judge you; he came to save you. Out of God's love for you, he seeks to remove the things that separate you from him. And one of the main things that separates you from God is the shame and condemnation you embrace because of your sin.

The only way to diminish the power of shame is to embrace the unfailing love of God.

We have an option.

We can listen to shame. We can allow shame to tell us that God loves us less than he did before we messed up (or less than he loves other people). We can let shame play our mistakes on repeat until they're literally all we can think about.

Or we can listen to the One who made us. We can believe his words about us. We can believe him when he says that his love is free, and that it has nothing to do with our behavior.

These realizations would not come to me until later in my recovery. They would not come to me in rehab. I wouldn't make these connections until much later—when I was willing to lay down my pride like Jesus laid down his life.

ELEVEN

Better Together

By what power did you do this? . . . And through whose name?

Acts 4:7

By this point in my story, I had been sick with a severe eating disorder for years. Not a day went by that I didn't obsess, monitor, and control my eating at a manic level. And since I had gone to treatment, everyone assumed that I was all well and good.

That's not to say that anyone—including my parents—didn't do all they could to assure that I was staying on track. They did. They gave me more support and encouragement than any other parents could give. It's just that I had a whole new skill set now. I had learned the words and phrases of recovery without ever having to actually practice it. I was better at hiding my secret now.

And then I met Brad Hughes.

Isn't even his name just the most attractive thing ever?

I met Brad when I was twenty years old, working at Fellowship Church's main campus in Grapevine, Texas. Well, that's not exactly how it happened. I should say that Brad met *me*. I sort of, kind of (definitely), stalked him and orchestrated the whole ordeal.

It all started with an Instagram post.

I know, I know. I've spent a lot of time in this book talking about how we shouldn't let social media drive our actions.

But here's the thing. In this instance, I definitely let social media drive my actions.

Do with that what you wish. It's just the truth.

Anyway, Brad's sister Bri and her husband, Eric, were on staff at the church. Brad was living in Indiana and working for his dad when he visited Dallas to stay with Bri and Eric while he went to a nearby youth conference. And like the proud sister that she is, Bri posted a picture on Instagram of herself and Brad at the airport.

And like any good Insta-stalker, I even commented on the picture in hopes that he would see it, click on my profile, and fall madly in love with me. Because, let me tell you—that boy is fiiiine. I mean, he is easy on the eyes for days and days and days. Like, Greek-god level good-looking. (Okay, I'll stop now.)

One of the days that Brad was in town, he stopped by the church to hang out in the office area where we do a lot of our service planning. When I caught wind of this news, I immediately found a pressing matter that needed my personal attention. In those same offices.

I remember walking in and seeing him in person for the first time. He was every inch of six-foot-seven, and when he shook my hand, I probably said something ridiculous and completely inarticulate. There were two other girls in the room with us, and it was all I could do to keep from jumping up in his arms like a damsel in distress to mark my territory. I can laugh about it now, but it really was borderline ridiculous.

After that connection, I just *knew* he was going to ask Bri about me and promptly ask me to marry him.

When Brad *didn't* see my comment, click on my profile, and fall in love with me, and he *didn't* ask his sister about me and have a ring on layaway, I took matters into my own hands. I texted Bri and said something like, "Girl. Your brother is so cute." I know. I'm impressed with my own maturity and wit. So Bri and I texted back and forth, and we wound up making plans for dinner in hopes that Brad would join us.

Aaaaaand that's exactly what happened.

The three of us went to what is now Brad's and my favorite Mexican restaurant at the West Village in Dallas and basically held Bri hostage while we talked for hours and hours and hours over burritos and enchiladas.

After that, I just knew. I just knew I was going to marry him.

We spent the next few months in a long-distance relationship, which we both hated. But like a lot of things, in hindsight, I see how *good* it was for me. For us. It forced Brad and me to take things much slower than we would have had he been local. (Although we did FaceTime each other literally all night long, from six o'clock in the evening until the sun came up and the birds were chirping outside.)

Fueled by coffee and that giddy, good anxiousness of knowing I'd found something *real*, I fell in love with Brad. He is steady. He is safe. He loves God. And he loved me.

The night my twin sister got married, Brad and I walked away from the party to talk alone. It was a cool December evening, and I remember just wanting to wrap my arms around his broad shoulders and never let go. (We're still newlyweds, so feel free to gag!) The reception music floated down to where we were standing, the sun was setting, and the sound of our loved ones' laughter filled the space between us and the wedding.

"I love you," Brad told me. And I felt the weight of his words down in the deepest part of my soul. "I am going to marry you, Landra."

And I can't explain it. I can't even begin to describe it. But in that moment, the Holy Spirit filled me with such a burning, overflowing compulsion that I literally could *not* keep my mouth shut any longer.

Because the thing was, Brad did love me. But he only knew *part* of me. And I couldn't let a man marry me unless he knew exactly what he was signing up for. I had this whole entire other side of my life and myself that Brad knew nothing (or very little) about. Because how could he really *love* me if he didn't really *know* me?

Until that point, fear had held me back from being completely vulnerable with him. It had become my thoughtless impulse to put on the "I am fine" mask and pretend like I was well, so it wasn't that I intentionally misled Brad. But at the same time, I wasn't being fair to him either. I wasn't giving him the chance to show me grace and to exercise the mercy he and I claimed to embrace on a weekly basis as active Christ followers.

Before the moment passed me by, I opened my mouth and told Brad the truth. I told him everything. Every detail. Every secret. I confessed to him that I was a liar, that I was sick, and that I needed help—real help.

First of all, if you don't believe in the power of confession, I've got to tell you—it's real.

I always forget that Jesus had a brother named James. I wonder what *that* dynamic was like. Like, *you* think *you* don't measure up when it comes to your family members, try being a sibling to God's only Son.

What if your brother claimed to be the Messiah? I mean, my brother is amazing but seriously? We see the worst of the worst when it comes to family members we grow up with. So if James believed that Jesus was who he said he was, then none of us should really have any questions about Jesus's true character.

Anyway, James wrote a letter in the Bible that talks about the power of confession. You may have heard this verse about confession before, but I believe it's one of the underrated disciplines of the Christian faith. Listen to this: "So confess your sins to one another. Pray for one another so that you might be healed. The prayer of a godly person is powerful. Things happen because of it" (James 5:16).

Confess your sins to one another. Yes, that sounds terrifying. Yes, that sounds risky. Yes, that sounds sort of like standing naked in Times Square with a spotlight on you. But it's also the single pathway to our emotional and spiritual freedom.

There are several reasons confessing our sins one to another is key in our healing. For one, our words have power. Our words can hurt. Our words can bless. We were created in God's image—not just from his thoughts but from the words that he used. He spoke and created us and the universe in which we live. When he said, "Let there be light," light appeared. We may not be able to speak galaxies into existence, but like our Creator, our words can build up and they can tear down.

Words are the way God works—our faith is built on this principle. Hebrews 11:3 puts it this way:

We have faith. So we understand that everything was made when God commanded it. That's why we believe that what we see was not made out of what could be seen.

And how did God command it? Out loud. With his words. Words are also spiritual. Our salvation requires some sort of confession.

Say with your mouth, "Jesus is Lord." Believe in your heart that God raised him from the dead. Then you will be saved. With your heart you believe and are made right with God. With your mouth you say what you believe. And so you are saved. (Rom. 10:9–10)

I love what James says about the power of our tongues.

And how about ships? They are very big. They are driven along by strong winds. But they are steered by a very small rudder. It makes them go where the captain wants to go. In the same way, the tongue is a small part of a person's body. But it talks big. (James 3:4–5)

Our tongues—what they say and don't say—steer the direction of our entire lives. Our words are like the stepping-stones we move across from conversation to conversation, moving us with their weight and importance. Our words hold a supernatural power—power that alters circumstances and shapes fates.

Have you ever thought about the fact that humans are the only creation that has the unique ability to speak words? Because of this ability, we have the power to communicate some pretty complicated and complex ideas and thoughts to one another. Our ability to talk—our ability to share our sins with one another—is not only a gift, it's a responsibility we have as people who believe in the power of confession.

Right after I confessed to Brad, he knelt with me and prayed for me. He thanked God for bringing us together. He thanked God for my courage to be honest. And he asked God to heal me and to help him navigate the coming days as we addressed my issues together.

While God was with me every step of my disease, I had never fully invited anyone else into my physical life to share in my pain.

Everything about my life started moving in a different direction the moment I confessed my sin and my sickness out loud.

Okay, before you start to hear me say you need a man to be healed, let's break down the crux of what I am saying.

Remember how we talked earlier about bringing what's in the dark into the light? How when we do that, the darkness loses its power?

When I went to rehab, it was like me barely edging my toes into the sunlight. I moved closer to bringing my darkness out in the open light, but there was still a lot of me left in the shadows.

But that night with Brad, I was different. It was like I was baking in the sunshine. (I would like to say it was like basking in the sunshine, but there was nothing comfortable or relaxing about telling the man I loved that I had an entire life he knew nothing about.) I told him every single bit of what I was still struggling with. I exposed my secret in the most graphic, pointed way I ever had before. Maybe it was the first time I was admitting the depth of it to myself, even.

And in that moment, in the way that only God facilitates, I experienced a supernatural healing that a million words on a million pages couldn't describe.

Don't hear me say that I went home that night and never struggled with my eating disorder ever again, because that certainly wasn't the case. It was more like the net of lies I would wind around myself had been cut. I still find myself untangling pieces of that net from my life, but it no longer has the power to imprison me.

Because I had someone in the trenches with me. It was easier to get well when we did it *together*—a far, far more manageable goal than doing it alone. Healing is done better when it's done *together*.

But that is true about most things in life, right? Think about it. Going to the movies by yourself? Not that awesome. Taking a solo vacation? Though it may sound pretty nice in theory, the reality is it'd probably get lonely and monotonous. And it would just be *more fun* with someone you love alongside you. What about going to a football game? How much better is it to be sitting side by side with a friend and fellow fan, cheering on your favorite team?

Basically, the only thing that *isn't* done better together is a trip to Target in the middle of the week. Those trips are always, always done best alone.

Even as adults, don't we text each other to see if our friends are going to be somewhere?

"Are you going to Curriculum Night at the kids' school?"

"Will I see you at the church luncheon?"

"You planning to be at Kate's birthday party?"

Because honestly, the idea of walking into a new place without a familiar or friendly face is just as terrifying to me as a grown-up as it was when I was in middle school.

Part of what makes having a twin such an amazing experience is that, for at least the first part of your life, you really never *have* to be by yourself. From the womb on, I've been conditioned to do things *together*. That is why I am convinced one of the main contributing factors that made rehab such a traumatic experience was walking into a building where I knew literally no one. To *live*. Never had I felt (or physically been) so alone.

That feeling of having a person by your side can be one of the best feelings in the world. Everything is more fun, not to mention less awkward. I also believe that having a person by your side can give you courage. I mean, who goes skydiving alone? Who goes bungee jumping alone? Who goes parasailing alone?

(If your answer to any of those questions is, "Oh, I do!" then you are an incredibly brave, independent individual and I salute you!)

I know these things to be true, and yet, I was so unwilling to invite anyone into my healing.

But we do that, right? Sometimes, when we're hurting, lonely, or scared, we isolate ourselves. We tell ourselves that parties, events, and outings are better when done together, but when it comes to *hard* stuff, especially faith stuff, we feel like we're on our own.

When it comes to the inner workings of our hearts, we go it alone.

We pray alone.

We read the Bible alone.

We battle insecurity alone.

We wrestle with God alone.

We have doubts and questions and uncertainties that we struggle with alone.

Why? Why do we choose to be alone on these crucial, life-altering situations when we don't even want to go to a kid's birthday party alone?

For me, it all came down to *fear*. And we'll talk more about that in the next chapter, but I want you to think about what that answer is for you.

Maybe you keep your personal life private because that's what's been modeled for you. Maybe your parents never talked about spiritual or faith-based topics and it's just a foreign concept to you.

Maybe it feels weird to let others in when you have doubts because you are afraid of looking stupid or weak or like you're not a "good" Christian.

Or maybe it's because you aren't even sure how to begin to invite others into this part of your life. It may not be that you are intentionally keeping people out of your faith. It just may be you don't know *how* it could look any different for us.

If we're honest, I think we'd all say that we have a natural tendency to keep our faith journey a personal one. Even if we've gone to church our entire lives, even if we post Scripture on social media daily, and even if we attend every conference Beth Moore has ever put on. For the most part, we'd say that our convictions, our struggles, our doubts, our victories, and our failures all happen alone. What's that all about? If we know that every other area of life is better with others in it, why do we hesitate to do the hard work of faith by ourselves? And beyond that, how did we convince ourselves that that's how God intended it to be?

If you've been a Christian for any amount of time, you know that the Church (everyone who follows Jesus and his teachings) started with a bunch of people living their lives together.

Like, literally together. They shared everything—food, clothes, shelter. And they especially shared their faith, because their faith was the biggest driving force in their decision making. Fast-forward to today, when distractions from our soul-health are literally a smartphone away, and I think we (at least *I*) have lost sight of the importance of sharing our faith with those around us (not in an evangelical way but in a "let's do real life together" way).

For me, learning to do this—to live out what I believe honestly and openly—has been critical in my learning to trust others and in learning to trust (and love) myself.

Instead of telling you what I think, let's look at the people who got this right *without* the technological capabilities that we have today. (For instance, I am pretty sure they "went to the restroom" in a hole in the ground. If they can figure out a way to successfully do community, we really don't have an excuse, right?)

Obviously, we're going to look at some Scriptures from the book of Acts. If you aren't that familiar with the Bible, there ain't no shame in that. Basically, the book of Acts is the book of Luke, part two. It talks about Jesus's time on earth and in particular, about the acts of Jesus's followers, the apostles.

The last thing Jesus told his friends (and us!) to do was to go and tell the world about him. Seems simple enough.

Luke was a doctor. He wrote the book of Luke and the book of Acts as a letter to a guy named Theophilus. Luke had one major goal in these writings, and that was to convince Theophilus that Jesus was who he said he was and did what people were saying he had done. And I don't know if Luke wrote this way because he was a doctor or because that was just his wiring, but he communicated in great detail. (And, honestly, if someone was writing me a letter about the death and resurrection of a guy who claimed to be the Son of God, I would probably want a little description myself.)

Because he was a skilled healer and a skilled writer, Luke presented a clear and compelling case regarding the validity of Jesus's claims, and he also painted a picture of the cultural response to Jesus and his followers. It's because of Luke's meticulous record that we have an idea of just how dramatically the first-century world changed in response to the ministry and life of Jesus. And we also get a feel for the history and the emotion surrounding the beginnings of the Jesus-following movement.

So back to our example of sharing faith from Acts.

Obviously, none of us can imagine what life was like for the people living during that time. Not only because it was two thousand–plus years ago but also because some significantly crazy stuff had just gone down. The apostles (or disciples) had been following Jesus for *years*. Doing life with him. Hanging out with him. Sharing meals with him. They had an idea of what Jesus would do, but they didn't know his plan *exactly*. During this time, the Hebrew people were ruled by some pretty hard-core Roman leaders. It's likely the disciples thought Jesus would intervene on a governmental level and start an uprising.

But that's not what happened.

Instead, Jesus was arrested. And then he was murdered in public.

Sidebar: have you ever gotten this idea in your mind about how you'll be freed, healed, or fulfilled, and it literally went the opposite direction? Like, not only were your hopes of something better completely obliterated but the situation actually got *worse*? Yeah, that's the boat the disciples were in.

But that's the thing about God. He wants to know if we're brave enough, and faithful enough, to make it through that last hour of complete darkness before the sun rises on our doubts, fears, and losses.

The religious leaders hated Jesus. (They literally wanted him dead, so it doesn't get a lot more hateful than that.) And essentially, it all boiled down to jealousy. Can you imagine being so envious of someone that you would actually plot and execute their death? Go ahead and pat yourselves on the back. Finally, something in the Bible that makes us feel good about ourselves! (Okay, that was a joke. I love the Bible. It's filled with incredible, encouraging words about us. But sometimes reading about biblical heroes can leave me feeling a little less than award-winning!)

Anyway, after Jesus was crucified, his former besties-for-the-resties did what any of the rest of us would do—they ran! They scattered, terrified of what the murder of their leader and friend meant for them, their families, and their faith. They abandoned their homes. They abandoned one another.

But then a rumor started circulating. A rumor that someone had seen Jesus . . . after his death. A rumor that the tomb Jesus had been buried in—a tomb only two of the disciples visited and saw with their own eyes—had been reported as empty. At first, they thought the Romans had taken the body, either out of fear that Jesus's followers would try to do the same, or for some further, perverse punishment.

Not even Jesus's own followers expected that it could actually be something completely different. No one expected that the unexpected had happened. No one even uttered the word *resurrection*. No one even guessed that Jesus was actually alive.

But then—and I want you to picture this—eleven of the twelve original disciples got together. They were all gathered in a room when they learned that Jesus was not dead. That, in fact, he was very much alive, having appeared to Peter, John, and to Mary Magdalene. And then . . . Jesus SHOWED UP. I don't think we can wrap our minds around that. I know I can't. To borrow a line from *The Bachelor*, it was THE MOST SHOCKING REVEAL EVER!

Apparently, the whole coming-back-to-life thing was a pretty convincing act because many, many new followers were added to the church following Jesus's resurrection. So for the next forty days, Jesus spent time with the disciples and with the new followers. But it was never Jesus's intention to stay on earth. In the beginning of Acts, Jesus ascends to heaven and leaves his friends and followers. In his stead, they receive the Holy Spirit, just like Jesus promised they would.

But the rest—the rest of their faith journey—was up to them.

Though I am sure they were still scared, or at least a little nervous, the disciples moved forward with a renewed boldness. They started preaching, they started healing, and they started doing whatever it took to obey Jesus's final command to go out and spread the word and love of their heavenly Father to as many people as possible.

And that's where we pick up, in Acts 4.

The Bible tells us that Jesus was especially close with three of his disciples. Two of them, Peter and John, headline our story. They were talking about Jesus to a crowd of people who had gathered to listen—sort of like an impromptu church service.

That was a pretty risky move, considering the religious leaders were angrier than ever that the Way was continuing without Jesus at its (physical) helm.

And, yup. Sure enough, just as Peter and John were getting wound up preaching, the priests of the temple showed up to call them out. And in true Roman-temple-priest fashion, Peter and John were arrested. I am sure no one was rushing to get them before a judge, but it was later in the day. So Peter and John were thrown in jail to be dealt with the following morning.

The sun rose and Peter and John were dragged in front of a council of rulers, teachers, and elders—you know, just the super important people of that time. (a.k.a. the key players in Jesus's assassination). If I had been Peter or John, I would have been pleading the fifth. Actually, I would have been pleading the whatever-kept-me-alive.

So when Peter and John were finally brought before the super scary council, here's what they were asked: "By what power did you do this? . . . And through whose name?" (Acts 4:7).

In other words, what gives you the right to *continue* with this Jesus-is-God's-Son garbage we've done everything possible to squash? Have we not been clear? Did murdering your "King" send a mixed signal?

Again, to reiterate, I would be running for my life. But Peter went and did a very *Peter* thing. He began talking about the miracles that they had been performing. And he reasoned that their ability to perform such acts could only come one way.

He said to them, "Rulers and elders of the people! Are you asking us to explain our actions today? Do you want to know why we were kind to a man who couldn't walk? Are you asking how he was healed? Then listen to this, you and all the people of Israel! You nailed Jesus Christ of Nazareth to the cross. But God raised him from the dead. It is through Jesus' name that this man stands healed in front of you." (Acts 4:8–10)

I sort of want to giggle when I read Peter's response. Peter was saying, "Are you *seriously* still asking these same questions?" Then he reminded them that they murdered Jesus. "Remember that guy? The one you KILLED?! That's the guy whose Holy Spirit empowers us to do these great works."

Scripture goes on to say how stunned the leaders were upon hearing this, because it was obvious Peter and John were just normal guys. They weren't doctors. Or priests. Or teachers. They had no special training and they didn't come from powerful or influential families, like many sitting on the council. So how could it be that their messages had reached such an incredible number of people and that they were accomplishing these amazing things? No one could figure out *how*. What was it about these guys that made them different? That gave them influence? That gave them the ability to *heal*?

The Bible says that the religious leaders were surprised. But that didn't mean that they were on board with Peter and John and their mission or ministry. It also didn't mean they agreed with what Peter and John were teaching.

I like this part, because we sort of get a sneak peek into what happened when the council convened to decide what they should do with them. Here's what they said:

"What can we do with these men?" they asked. "Everyone living in Jerusalem knows they have performed an unusual miracle.

We can't say it didn't happen. We have to stop this thing. It must not spread any further among the people. We have to warn these men. They must never speak to anyone in Jesus' name again." Once again the leaders called in Peter and John. They commanded them not to speak or teach at all in Jesus' name. (Acts 4:16–18)

Aaaaaand, I am sure you can guess how their "recommendation" went over with Peter and John.

But Peter and John replied, "Which is right from God's point of view? Should we listen to you? Or should we listen to God? You be the judges! There's nothing else we can do. We have to speak about the things we've seen and heard." (Acts 4:19–20)

For Peter and John, obeying the religious leaders wasn't an option. As Peter said, how could they *not* tell others what they'd seen and heard?

Well, the leaders didn't know what to do with that. They weren't used to people showing courage in the face of their threats, and they definitely weren't accustomed to people just straight up refusing to do what they said. Plus, there was the whole fact that what Peter and John were doing and saying was sort of undeniable. And even though the council hated to hear about it, the people in their communities *loved* it.

They were stuck. They wanted to punish Peter and John. They wanted to make an example out of them, just like they had with Jesus. But they couldn't. They knew that the people would rebel. They knew it would cause a riot they couldn't withstand. So what did they do? *They let Peter and John go.*

It's a pretty unbelievable turn of events. Especially when you remember the kind of people Peter and John used to be. The book of Luke tells us about Peter being asked about his association with Jesus the night he was arrested before being crucified. Peter was sitting around a fire when a girl asked him if he knew Jesus. And guess what Peter's reply was? "Who, me? Know Jesus? Nope." He denied it not once, twice, but *three* times. Ouch. (See Luke 22:56–61 for the whole story.)

Then, just months later, Peter was threatened with arrest, and he told the religious leaders, the most powerful people in the Hebrew community, he couldn't help but let people know about Jesus.

So what changed?

Obviously having the power of the Holy Spirit was a difference-maker. But that wasn't all. They also had each other. In fact, when Peter and John were freed by the council, they went back to the group of new believers that had been forming. They told them what had happened—they told them that the religious leaders had demanded a cease and desist on the Jesus stuff. And do you know what the group's response was?

They prayed. Together. In the face of being arrested, thrown in jail, and possibly being killed, their collective courage spurred them forward. And because of that, you and I got to hear about Jesus, and our kids will hear about Jesus, and their kids will hear about Jesus.

Aren't you glad Jesus's disciples and the early church decided to share their faith with one another? Aren't you grateful that once his chosen disbanded, Jesus brought them back together to combine forces to tell others about his Father?

I am. Because the truth is, we're better together. We're better individuals, we're better leaders—we're just better people.

So what does this mean for us? We may not be out risking our lives to share the name of Jesus. But if you're anything like me, when you're afraid, you don't run to a friend and ask them to help make you brave. Instead, you obsess. You isolate yourself. You get on Instagram and start to make assessments about yourself in comparison to others' highlight reels.

We've gotta knock it off. We've just got to. If we want to love ourselves—and more than that, if we want to experience the fullness of what God has for us—we have to link arms with one another. We have to share our lives and share our faith. We have to find like-minded friends who challenge us to stand up to our fears. And maybe your fears *do* feel as daunting as facing the Roman council. Maybe your fears include:

confronting a family member
ending a toxic relationship
battling cancer
asking for forgiveness
moving to a different state or country
dealing with an eating disorder

Whatever your Roman council is, you don't have to face it alone. In fact, you shouldn't.

People have asked me—Landra, how did you get better? How did you find healing? What was the *one thing* that made the difference?

Yes, I told Brad the truth, allowing my darkness to be brought into the light. That was the moment I laid down my final bit of pride. And yes, recovering with someone in the trenches with me gave me a new level of strength and confidence.

But those were the tangibles.

The truth is, it was a hundred tiny choices I learned to make for myself that led me to recovery once I was finally ready to take the steps I needed to take.

I found healing in reading my Bible. In praying real (sometimes R-rated) prayers. In going to church and actually engaging in community. In going to therapy and confronting the ways I had allowed this disease to take root in me. In taking walks and intentionally thanking God for his creation. In practicing gratitude by writing down things I was thankful for. In slowing down. In saying no and meaning it. In saying yes and meaning it.

Through each small, often unnoteworthy step I took toward my heavenly Father, I slowly began to feel familiar with my Creator. He was no longer God in the sky, incomprehensible and complicated. But he became a friend—beside me and with me, hand in hand.

I began to expect—according to his character—good things, even when I didn't see them. I found that his love for me was immeasurable and unconditional.

When I fell in love with God, I was also able to fall in love with me.

TWELVE

A Different Kind of Love Story

Who can separate us from Christ's love? Can trouble or hard times or harm or hunger? Can nakedness or danger or war? . . . No! In all these things we are more than winners! We owe it all to Christ, who has loved us.

Romans 8:35, 37

When's the last time you went to the beach? I love the beach, but I'll never forget my most recent trip. I was hanging with my family and some good friends. One of my friends brought an inflatable raft, so I took it out in the shallow water to make my lack of a tan a little less offensive to the general public. Or, at least, that was my plan. I made sure someone had an eye on Sterling, then I lay down on the raft and closed my eyes.

And like any other exhausted mom of a toddler, closing my eyes for ten seconds turned into an unintentional ten-minute power nap. I lifted my head to realize that not only was I FAR away from the beach but I was also what seemed like a mile down the shoreline. It was crazy. And obviously the ocean is filled with terrifying monsters like jellyfish, so I started freaking out.

Without even realizing it, I had been caught in a riptide. Has that ever happened to you? You can even be standing in the water and slowly float down the beach without knowing. It's crazy! I mean, I was lucky that I had a raft keeping me afloat, but I can't tell you how PANICKED I was when I woke up. First of all, naps are disorienting enough but it's also a pretty helpless feeling to be at the mercy of the ocean.

Doesn't that kind of feel like our life sometimes?

Like we're just floating out in the middle of the ocean, at the mercy of its riptide?

God's will is complex and I often have questions.

Why are there kids with cancer?

Why are there people who are born with a compulsion to abuse children?

Why are there genetic disorders?

Why are there mass shootings in elementary schools?

Why do bad things happen to good people?

Anytime we're not happy with ourselves, anytime we are stressed out or lonely, or anytime we're going through something painful, it can feel a lot like we're on a runaway raft, being dragged along the ocean by some invisible force that we can't see or control. It can feel like God's will has been overridden by some more powerful, more subversive will. A will that wants us to lose.

It's during these times that it's incredibly difficult to feel good about who we are. Because if we were good people, wouldn't our lives *look* good? Wouldn't they *feel* good? Wouldn't they *be* good?

In elementary school, one of my favorite teachers passed away from cancer. In middle school, a classmate of mine also passed away from cancer. In high school, a girl on my baseball team died in a car accident. Each time I faced these tragedies, some big fears dominated my mind—all centering on three questions.

1. **Will it ever end?** Whether the tragedy is happening to us or we're watching it happen to someone else, we all wonder: *Will this pain ever fade? Will it always feel as bad as it feels right now?*

2. **Will it happen to me?** I never thought about dying from cancer until my friend passed away. Then I thought about it a lot.

3. **Will it happen again?** Growing up, I thought about this when I saw tragedies of all sorts. In fact, I still think about it today. There's a fear in the back of my mind that I'm never completely safe, and neither are the people I care about.

Even worse, I remember feeling totally aimless and disconnected from the one person who mattered most. The one person who I thought was most capable of doing something about the darkness I was facing—God.

In the middle of a tragedy, most people want to ask this question: God, where are you?

When you're in the middle of a time of darkness, it challenges your ability to trust God like nothing else can. In addition, it messes with your emotions. You may *know* something in your head, but what you *feel* may seem to go against everything you once thought was true.

In a lot of ways, things that once seemed stable suddenly feel completely out of control . . . just like being caught in a riptide that's pulling you away from where you want to be.

That's why I'm ending this book by talking about having an anchor. The passage we're going to look at together can offer you just that when it comes to walking through the darkness. And it could potentially change the way you see pain, the way you see yourself, and the way you see God in the middle of it.

We've talked a lot about Paul. He's obviously one of my favorites. After his first encounter with God, Paul spent his entire life getting the message of Jesus out to as many people as possible.

In the first century, Paul wrote a letter to the church in Rome. During that time, Rome was a powerhouse empire. You've heard the word *empire* before, but I'm not sure any of us have context for what that really means. When I say empire, I don't just mean a really powerful country. Rome had complete control over much of the world. And they didn't play around—getting on the wrong side of the Roman Empire meant you'd die painfully. So during that time, people would generally keep a low profile and just go with the flow. But the church and the Roman Empire didn't exactly see eye to eye.

The emperor of Rome at the time was Nero. Many people believe that Nero had a strong hatred for Christians and even went so far as to torture and execute them. So it's safe to assume the Christians in Rome were really familiar with tragedy—they probably lived in constant fear of tragedy striking them or their loved ones.

At the time Paul wrote this letter, he was about to travel to Jerusalem—knowing in advance that, because of his outspoken faith, his life would be in danger there. Some people believe Paul wrote his letter to the Romans believing it was the last thing he would write.

So when you read the following words, understand they weren't written—or read—on a lounge chair beside a pool. They were written from the darkness of fear and pain. For the writer and the reader, life was *very* unstable. Tragedy was real and personal. And with those circumstances in mind, Paul wrote this: "What should we say then? Since God is on our side, who can be against us?" (Rom. 8:31).

When Paul says, "What should we say," he's talking about what a believer's response should be to suffering. Pain. Heartache. Tragedy.

Then he makes an interesting statement. "Since God is on our side, who can be against us?"

When tragedy strikes, we don't know how to respond. We don't know what to do. We ask big and heavy questions. We feel isolated, devastated, hopeless, and unmoored.

And in response, Paul gives us the answer. It doesn't feel like an answer though; it feels like he ignored our questions completely. But Paul says that when tragedy happens, when pain happens, when you're going through the darkness, remember what God has already done for you.

He gave us Jesus. Jesus, who put on human flesh and experienced pain, hurt, loss, and even death *with* us. In the death of his own Son, God entered into our pain, tragedy, and hurt.

Our hurt doesn't surprise him, and it's not foreign to him. He is *with* us in our darkness.

But God isn't just in it *with* us. Paul says God is *for* us. He did not spare his own Son; instead, he gave his Son so that we would have an incredible promise to hold on to. Here's how Paul said it:

> Who can separate us from Christ's love? Can trouble or hard times or harm or hunger? Can nakedness or danger or war? . . . No! In all these things we are more than winners! We owe it all to Christ, who has loved us. (Rom. 8:35, 37)

When Jesus rose from the dead, he defeated the darkness. And he didn't just defeat the darkness for himself. He did it for us. He defeated OUR darkness. And because he conquered the darkness, we can too. We are, as Paul said, more than conquerors. And it's not because we're able to get a grip on darkness and figure it out. No, it's because God has a grip on us. And nothing is ever going to separate us from him. According to Paul,

> I am absolutely sure that not even death or life can separate us from God's love. Not even angels or demons, the present or the future, or any powers can separate us. Not even the highest places or the lowest, or anything else in all creation can separate us. Nothing at all can ever separate us from God's love. That's because of what Christ Jesus our Lord has done. (Rom. 8:38–39)

You see, we live in a world full of darkness—a world where not everything is as it should be. But the one thing that remains strong and steady is the love of God.

When you're going through darkness—darkness of any sort—just remember that *nothing* can separate you from the God who loves you.

No matter how threatening the pain. No matter how slippery or scary the conditions. When we wonder, *Where's God in all of this?* He's there. And his love proves it.

Here's something that I've learned a lot about, especially recently. God being *with* us doesn't mean the pain isn't *with* us. God and pain can and do exist in the same scenarios. The thing to remember is that God is right there with you—sitting in the middle of your mess, your pain, and your darkness.

The Christians in Rome had the same question back then that we have today: Where is God when terrible things happen? And the answer is the same now as it was then. You can't be separated from him. So you can face whatever happens.

Even if it feels like it will never end, you can persevere because God is with you.

Even if you're scared it will happen to you, you can trust that God is with you and he cares for you. He won't let go of you.

Even if you're afraid it will happen again, God is with you now and he'll be with you then—no matter what.

A tragedy might separate you from a loved one, but it can't separate you from God's love. A divorce might separate you from a member of your family, but it can't separate you from God's presence. Sickness might separate you from health, but it cannot separate you from the comfort of your heavenly Father. Nothing can separate you from the God who loves you.

Your fear, your worry, and your uncertainty in what comes next do not compare to what we know to be true. God's love is bigger. And he is for you.

This doesn't make tragedy easy to go through. It doesn't answer all our questions. And it doesn't guarantee an easier life. In fact, Emperor Nero eventually took Paul's life. But even as he died, Paul held on to this anchor. Even when he felt devastated, he never felt hopeless. Because he knew God was beside him every step of the way.

I wish I could tell you that I haven't struggled a single day since surrendering my eating disorder to God. But that wouldn't be true. In fact, in the last few months, I've struggled more than normal. Brad and I have moved two times, started a new church campus, and my family has experienced a deep, crushing tragedy that is still too fresh to talk about.

There are times that I eat like I'm supposed to. And then there are times that I don't. Do you want to know what's helped? Writing this book. The message of this book is FOR ME. I need to hear these words, because they're founded in God's Holy Word.

You are not alone in your darkness.

As I've said throughout this book, there's no quick or easy answer when you're dealing with tough or tragic times. But that doesn't mean there's no hope. There *is* something you can do in the darkness. It may seem simple at first, but it's extremely powerful.

You can create an anchor.

If you're on a boat in the middle of a storm, an anchor can keep your boat from drifting. It can help you maintain the right direction against the wind. It can keep you stabilized while everything else swirls around like madness.

In the same way, when you're going through the darkness, you need something to hold on to. Something solid—a phrase or an idea—that can provide a dose of hope when you're feeling hopeless. Something that brings peace when you're afraid and security when you're anxious. So when you're hurting, find a truth to hold on to. And hold on to it as tightly as you can. Write it down. Put it on the lock screen of your phone. Put it on a notecard and tape it to your bathroom mirror. Don't just create an anchor—hold on to it!

The truth I anchored in myself is one of the simplest, most basic principles of the Christian faith. But the depth of its meaning, the implications of its truth, the reverberations of its greatness, they're my *anchor* now. The thing that keeps me grounded, keeps me stable, keeps me well. And it's this—nothing can separate me from the God who loves me.

When we get this—when we wallow in the miraculous nature of his unconditional love—then and only then can we experience the kind of love we've been searching for our whole lives.

It's only when we trust in the unfailing, unchanging, unyielding, unconditional love of our heavenly Father that we can trust, like, and love his creation—ourselves.

It's a different kind of love story.

It's not one that you'll watch on TV.

No one's going to give you a rose.

You won't need a cocktail dress or heels to win the prize.

It's a different kind of love story. It's *the* love story. And nothing can separate you from it.

ACKNOWLEDGMENTS

First of all, I want to thank my amazing husband. I wouldn't be where I am today without his love and support through every circumstance. My heart will always belong to you, Brad!

I also want to thank my incredible family. The love and support they have shown me through this entire season has meant more than words can say. Through all the hard times and good times, they have never given up on me and have always been there to remind me who God has created me to be.

And to Natalie, a woman who helped me find myself when I couldn't. I am so grateful. You have understood me and helped me find purpose in pain.

I also want to thank those who have stood beside me through all the hills and valleys of life—those who prayed for me when I didn't know what to pray for. Those who listened to me when I could barely put sentences together.

NOTES

Chapter 1 Plot Twist

1. Sean Sposato, "Na'vi language creator gives insight on the words within The World of Avatar in a visit to Pandora," InsidetheMagic.com, November 10, 2017, https://insidethemagic.net/2017/11/navi-language-creator-gives-insight-words-within-world-avatar-visit-pandora/.

Chapter 5 The Thief

1. Steve Weisman, "Is Identity Theft Protection Worth It?" *USA Today*, April 22, 2017, https://www.usatoday.com/story/money/columnist/2017/04/22/identity-theft-protection-worth/100554362/.

2. "Grasping Large Numbers," *Endowment for Human Development*, accessed August 20, 2019, https://www.ehd.org/science_technology_large numbers.php.

Chapter 6 Tell Me Lies

1. Marg Mowczko, "A Suitable Helper (in Hebrew)," *Margaret Mowczko* (blog), March 8, 2010, https://margmowczko.com/a-suitable-helper/.

2. Paraphrased from John H. Walton, *Genesis*, NIV Application Commentary (Grand Rapids: Zondervan, 2001), 176.

Chapter 7 Hope Is the Thing with Feathers

1. Emily Dickinson, "'Hope' is the thing with feathers- (314)," *Poetry Foundation*, accessed August 20, 2019, https://www.poetryfoundation.org/poems/42889/hope-is-the-thing-with-feathers-314. From *The Poems of Emily Dickinson*, ed. R. W. Franklin (Cambridge, MA: Harvard University Press, 1999).

2. Jerome Groopman, *The Anatomy of Hope: How People Prevail in the Face of Illness* (New York: Random House, 2004), xvi.

3. Groopman, *Anatomy of Hope*, xvi.

4. Amanda Enayati, "How Hope Can Help You Heal," *CNN Health*, April 11, 2013, https://www.cnn.com/2013/04/11/health/hope-healing-enayati/index.html.

5. Enayati, "How Hope Can Help You Heal."

Chapter 8 Have a Little Faith

1. For more "*Bachelor*-isms," visit https://www.theodysseyonline.com/33-sayings-you-hear-every-bachelor-episode.

2. "We're All Healed by Their Faith," Let Us Reason Ministries, accessed August 20, 2019, http://www.letusreason.org/Wf16.htm.

Landra Young Hughes is the daughter of prominent pastor Ed Young Jr. and Lisa Young of Fellowship Church. Because of her upbringing, Landra has developed a passion for seeing people maximize their God-given potential and embrace their God-defined self-worth. She and her husband, Brad, lead Fellowship Church's Norman campus and live in the Norman, Oklahoma, area with their daughter, Sterling.

Learn More about
FELLOWSHIP CHURCH

FELLOWSHIPCHURCH.COM